Guided Mindfulness Meditations & Bedtime Stories for Busy Adults: Beginners Meditation Scripts & Stories For Deep Sleep, Insomnia, Stress-Relief, Anxiety, Relaxation& Depression

By Meditation Made Effortless

Table of Contents

DAY 1—LEARNING TO BE CALM [5 MINUTES] 1

DAY 2—BREATHING INTO RELAXATION [5 MINUTES] ... 3

DAY 3—WINDING DOWN THE DAY [5 MINUTES] 5

DAY 4—LUNCHTIME RELAXATION MEDITATION [10 MINUTES] 7

DAY 5—MORNING MOOD BOOSTER MEDITATION [10 MINUTES] 10

DAY 6—QUICK ANXIETY REDUCING RELAXATION [10 MINUTES] 13

DAY 7—10 MINUTE PANIC ATTACK RELAXATION [10 MINUTES] 16

DAY 8—DEEP RELAXATION [15 MINUTES] 20

DAY 9—SUNSET MINDFULNESS [15 MINUTES] 24

DAY 10—AFTER WORK STRESS-RELIEVING MEDITATION [15 MINUTES] 27

DAY 11—PAUSING FOR RELAXATION [15 MINUTES] ... 31

DAY 12—THE ALERTNESS MEDITATION [15 MINUTES] 34

DAY 13—CALMING AFTER A PANIC ATTACK [15 MINUTES] 38

DAY 14—EASY-TO-FOLLOW SELF-HEALING MEDITATION [20 MINUTES] 42

DAY 15—SELF-CONFIDENCE MEDITATION [20 MINUTES] 47

DAY 16—THANKFULNESS AFTER A FULL DAY [20 MINUTES]..................52

DAY 17—DEALING WITH HEAVY EMOTIONS [20 MINUTES]..................57

DAY 18—THE DARKNESS AND INTO NOTHINGNESS [20 MINUTES]..................62

DAY 19—FLOATING ON WATER [20 MINUTES]............67

DAY 20—THE CANDLE MEDITATION EXERCISE [25 MINUTES]..................72

DAY 21—GUIDED MEDITATION FOR DEEP SLEEP [30 MINUTES]..................77

DAY 22—SELF-HEALING MEDITATION [30 MINUTES]..84

DAY 23—STRESS RELIEF MEDITATION: LOOKING AT THE STARS [30 MINUTES]..................91

DAY 24—BEFORE SLEEP DEEP RELAXATION MEDITATION: REFLECTING ON YOUR JOURNEY [30 MINUTES]..................98

DAY 25—RELAXED MINDFUL EATING: GUIDED MINDFULNESS TO APPRECIATE YOUR MEAL BETTER [30 MINUTES]..................105

DAY 26—MORNING ANXIETY-REDUCING MEDITATION TO KICK-START YOUR DAY [30 MINUTES]..................111

DAY 27—GUIDED MEDITATION FOR REDUCING ANXIETY: LISTENING TO THE WIND [30 MINUTES]..................118

DAY 28—STRESS-RELIEVING GUIDED MEDITATION— OVERCOMING CHRONIC FATIGUE [30 MINUTES]......124

DAY 29—STARING AT THE MONSTER & FACING THE ANXIETIES WITHIN: GUIDED MEDITATION TO OVERCOME ANXIETY [30 MINUTES] 131

DAY 30—GUIDED SLEEP MEDITATION: OFF TO LA-LA LAND... [40 MINUTES] 138

DAY 1—LEARNING TO BE CALM [5 MINUTES]

Welcome to your first day of guided mindfulness meditations. This book is perfect for busy people who are always on the go. This book aims to give guidance to each individual who looks for mindfulness and relaxation in their lives. By picking up this book, you are marching your way to a more mindful existence. You can look forward to relieving your stress, decreasing anxiety, and just feeling light.

For the very step of your journey, all you need to do is to learn how to calm yourself. That's about it. It seems as simple as it sounds, but it' actually very challenging. That's why you will be introduced to some key concepts that will help you with your mindfulness journey.

The first concept is to be 'in the here and now'.

What does this mean?

"Am I not in the here and now already?" you may be asking yourself.

Well, if you are beset with so many thoughts, if something is bothering you, if you seem to be unaware of what's happening in you and around you, then you are not in the here and now… Your body might be in the present… But your mind might be somewhere else… In the past, or somewhere far ahead in the future…

That is why you need to stop… Pause…

Close your eyes... Try to channel in the feeling of relaxation, of calm...

Then take a deep breath... As you do, try to block everything out... Just pause...

Maintain the deep breathing... Concentrate on it...

Think of your breathing as the only thing that matters now...

Take another deep breath...

Think of the words 'here' and 'now'....

Be in the here and now... And take in relaxation as you draw another breath...

Now... be in a state of calm...

DAY 2—BREATHING INTO RELAXATION [5 MINUTES]

As you learned the first key concept on day one, day two will introduce you to the technique that will greatly enhance your day one experience. Concentrating on your breathing is crucial to attaining relaxation. This will help you prime your mind so that you can achieve being in the 'here' and 'now' much faster.

Try to find a comfortable spot where you can have a few moments by yourself. Claim this spot as your own. You need your alone time to refocus, relax, decompress, and practice mindfulness. Settle into this spot and position your body in such a way that it will relaxed and calm. You may close your eyes as you do this exercise.

Take in a long and deep breath...

Breathe in... Hold... And then release...

Be very intentional as you draw and release your breath... Try to imagine the air going inside your nostrils and into your throat and windpipe... And finally, imagine the air settling inside your lungs... There it circulates for a few seconds... And then visualize it making its return voyage back to the outside...

Try to block out errant thoughts that may enter... Concentrate on visualizing your breathing... If thoughts do enter, then just let them be... Quickly acknowledge their presence and then let them pass... Continue visualizing your breath...

Breathe in... Hold... And then release...

Bring in relaxation as you inhale...

Breathe in... Hold... And then release...

Feel the calmness as oxygen fills your lungs...

Breathe in... Hold... And then release...

Relish at the calmness and peace you have achieved as you expel your breath...

Maintain the rhythm of your breathing... Continue to visualize the air that enters and leaves your body...

Be in the here and now...

And when you are ready to end your exercise, you may open your eyes...

DAY 3—WINDING DOWN THE DAY [5 MINUTES]

It's always great to have an opportunity to wind things down as the day comes to a close. After a hectic day, it's important to slow things down a bit. You will gain a deeper appreciation of your day if you take a few moments to reflect on it as it ends. This exercise will teach you how to slow down. It will let you revert the hyper-speed pace of life back down to normal speed. This is important as you gain a better understanding of yourself and of the world around you.

To begin, go back to your comfortable spot. The best time to do this is during sunset or as your workday is about to end. Go to your quiet spot to be alone. Make sure that this spot is free from your usual distractions. Try to disconnect from the outside world for a few moments, so turn off your mobile phone.

Start to take in a very deep breath... And close your eyes...

Breathe in... Hold... And then release...

Again, imagine the air that enters your body... See it in your mind's eye as it enters your body, penetrating each cell... See your breath bring you life-energy... And then see it flow out of you... bringing with it the cares and worries that you accumulated throughout the day...

Breathe in... Hold... And then release...

Breathe in... Hold... And then release...

Be in the here and now... In the here and now, time moves a little slower... You were running on hyper-speed earlier in the day... And that was needed for you to achieve your goals... Now that kind of rush is no longer needed... The workday is done... You don't need to run in fast-forward...

Go with the flow of time now... The pace is much slower... Your body is now still... It is getting more relaxed as it arrives in the here and now... Let your mind decelerate... Hit the brakes a little bit... Take it slow now...

Take it slow... Wind things down...

Let relaxation and calmness flow through you... This is what you need... This is what your body needs... And this is what your mind needs now...

Wind things down... Because the day is winding down as well... Time to get back to normal speed...

Breathe in... Hold... And then release...

As you get back to normal speed, feel free to make light movements. Feel and appreciate life at an unhurried pace... And then open your eyes...

DAY 4—LUNCHTIME RELAXATION MEDITATION [10 MINUTES]

This quick lunchtime relaxation meditation will offer you a respite that will bring your energies up as you tackle the second half of the day. It is important to be mindful of your energy level as the day progresses. There might be some mornings where, even though it's still early, your energies are already depleted. This exercise will help you replenish your energy as you go through your lunch break.

For this exercise, you need to find a place where you can be alone. Make sure that this place is somewhere free from distractions. It is best to go through this exercise away from other people so that you won't be bothered. So settle yourself and get comfortable so that you can begin.

Close your eyes... Try to release the tensions you are currently feeling...

You are on a break... This is the time where you can re-energize yourself... This is a time for you to pause... These few moments where you can achieve some form of rest from your break is crucial to your success later in the day...

Take in a long and deep breath...

Breathe in... Hold... And then release...

Visualize the air that you take in... Imagine it enter and leave your body... Visualize the air giving you a sense of lightness... It is making you feel more relaxed... Let the wonderful air flow inside of you... And then outside of you... In and out... In and out...

Breathe in... Hold... And then release...

You can feel your head feel light... Your neck and shoulders feel the same way too... It's like some burden is lifted off of it...

Your muscles are starting to relax as well... You can feel them slowly giving in to the lightness... This wonderful feeling energizes you... It reinvigorates your spirit...

Breathe in... Hold... And then release...

Be in the here and now... This is your time... This is the time for you to rest and recuperate... Maximize this time given to you...

Breathe in... Hold... And then release...

Good energy is starting to surround you... Let it ease away all tensions... Let it soften the tightness that you feel... Experience the good energy... And let all the negative energies flow out of you...

Breathe in... Hold... And then release...

You are in the here and now... In the here and now, the past and the future do not matter... In the here and now, you can recharge... Let your breathing recharge you... Feel the oxygen being distributed throughout your body... Feel your inner energies surge... Let this slow burn give you the energy you need for later...

Concentrate on your breathing... Concentrate on letting the good energy flow... This is how to be in the here and now...

Breathe in... Hold... And then release...

It's time to end your lunchtime relaxation meditation... It's time to face the day once again... Feel the surge of energy in your muscles. Do light movements, wiggle your fingers and toes, and then shake your arms and legs... This will let the energy flow through you. And then open your eyes. You are ready to face the rest of the day...

DAY 5—MORNING MOOD BOOSTER MEDITATION [10 MINUTES]

Mornings are the perfect time of day to boost your energy level. A great start to your day will usually ensure that you will finish your day strong. What's great about the morning is that you can have time for yourself to be alone, especially if you do this exercise really early. This mood booster will really help keep your energy levels high all throughout the day for superior performance.

For this exercise, it's advisable if you wake up early to do this. Go to your sweet spot from day one. Get comfortable. You can do this while still in your pajamas or sleepwear.

Let the stillness of the early morning bring you relaxation as you settle in to your comfortable position. And when you're ready to begin, close your eyes.

Start by concentrating on your breathing…

Breathe in… Hold… And then release…

Feel the freshness of the early morning air… Feel its vigor as it tries to wake you up… The air you breathe is full of energy… It is doing its best to energize each cell inside of you…

Visualize the air surrounding you… Try to see their form in your mind's eye… See the presence of this air and the energy it brings…Then imagine it entering your body as you inhale... And also imagine it going out of you as you exhale...

Breathe in... Hold... And then release...

Be intentional in your breathing... Focus on imagining your breath... Be as detailed as you can be... This is the only thing that matters now... In the early morning, it's just you and your breath....

Breathe in... Hold... And then release...

Be in the here and now... You are here where you find yourself... You are in your comfortable quiet place... And the now is the early morning... You took the time to be in your quiet place...

This thought brings you stillness and calmness... The here and now relaxes you... Because you know that the past and the future don't matter in the here and now... There will be another time and place for them... But not in the here and now...

In the here and now, it's just you and your breathing... That's what matters in the here and now... In the early morning, you are alone with your breath...

Breathe in... Hold... And then release...

Feel the rise in energy that is concurrently happening as the sun is starting its ascent... This is the power of the early morning... Feel the coolness of the air as it swirls around you... This is the coolness that the early morning gives... Notice the absence of noise... This is the kind of peace and quiet that the early morning offers...

This is the here and now that you find yourself in... Take it all in... Appreciate it... Let the early morning give you life... Let it give you the energy you will be needing for the day...

Breathe in... Hold... And then release...

It's time for you to start your day. Allow the morning to continue to bring you relaxation and energy. You can open your eyes when you're ready. And then get up—you should feel the energy flow through you now. Let this energy power you to success.

DAY 6—QUICK ANXIETY REDUCING RELAXATION [10 MINUTES]

Your anxieties come to you every so often without any announcement. They spring their attack suddenly and you are often caught by surprise. Sometimes, these anxieties are just there as you go through your day. They accumulate and build up until you can no longer take it and they start to spill over. That's why it's best to take some time to practice mindfulness and meditation in order to reduce you anxieties. This exercise will hopefully do just that.

You may do this exercise anytime you feel your anxieties starting to build up. You never know when you will have an anxiety attack. It's best to prevent these attacks by doing this exercise. Find a quiet and private space where you can be alone. Settle into a comfortable position and close your eyes.

The key to reducing anxiety is the notion of stopping. You need to stop. You need to pause. You need to cease whatever it was you were doing, whatever it was you were thinking… Just stop…. Pause…

As you close your eyes, try to become aware of the sensations that are trying to flood your senses… You might feel some weight on your head and shoulders… Your muscles might also be tensed… And there could also be butterflies in your stomach… Don't worry, these are all natural reactions to anxiety… This is your body telling you that it is experiencing anxiety just as your mind is experiencing it...

It is important to bring in awareness and focus on your breathing....

Breathe in... Hold... And then release...

Again, visualize your breath... Imagine the air as it enters your nostrils... Imagine the full details of this thought... Be very intentional in your breathing... Desire each breath... Really take time to feel it... Continue imagining your breath as it now reaches your lungs... See in your mind's eye your lungs enlarging with the presence of air... And then see your lungs distribute this oxygen to every cell in your body... And then it's time for this air to go out... Continue to imagine your lungs, this time it is contracting as it liberates itself from the air... And then imagine this air exiting from your nostrils as it rejoins the outside world...

Be very intentional in your breathing... Desire every breath... Know that this is the only thing that matters in the here and now... Because you are in the here and now...

Breathe in... Hold... And then release....

You are in the here and now... And in the here and now, your anxieties are far away....

Know that in the here and now, the past is no longer relevant... In the here and now, the future does not yet matter... Your anxieties are residents in the past and in the future... Therefore, they are either no longer relevant, or they still do not matter...

In the here and now, It's just you... and your breathing... In the here and now, you are calm... In the here and now, you are reclaiming lost energy... This was the energy you lost worrying over the past and the future... Reclaim all that energy you lost... It is yours for the taking, right here and right now...

Breathe in... Hold... And then release...

It's time to bring yourself back... Feel your body respond to the renewed energy... Slowly bring your senses back by making slow and measured movements... And once you're ready, open your eyes and get up. You will find yourself re-energized. You should also have renewed focus and your anxieties will have been greatly reduced.

DAY 7—10 MINUTE PANIC ATTACK RELAXATION [10 MINUTES]

You were on to a great start yesterday by learning how to reduce your anxieties. For this day, you will learn how to respond whenever you experience a panic attack. Sometimes, you will not be aware that you are already in the throes of a panic attack. What started out as a simple moment of fear might suddenly morph itself into a full blown panic attack. Panic attacks will cause you to freeze up. You will be debilitated by it. And it may be to your detriment because you will not know what to do. This exercise will hopefully free you from the clutches of panic.

This exercise can be done anytime and anywhere. After all, you cannot time panic attacks. So when you find yourself panicking, then you can activate this exercise.

Again, start by gaining awareness of yourself and the situation. If you find yourself overcome by great fear and this fear is starting to get in the way of you acting on it, then that could already be a panic attack. It is best to pause at this point. Stop what you are doing. Try to also stop whatever it is you were thinking. This is difficult to do, especially when you're already panicking. You can achieve this by concentrating on your breathing.

Concentrate on your breathing now...

Breathe in... Hold... And then release...

Be intentional... Be deliberate... You can ward off all those thoughts if you can build more awareness into your breathing...

Breathe in... Hold... And then release...

As you inhale, count one to four... As you do, picture out the numbers... Do the same when you hold your breath and when you exhale...

Breathe in... 1-2-3-4

Hold... 1-2-3-4

And then release... 1-2-3-4

Do it again... This time try to slow down your counting a bit...

Breathe in... 1... 2... 3... 4...

Hold... 1... 2... 3... 4...

And then release... 1... 2... 3... 4...

Be intentional in your breathing... Be intentional in trying to slow it down... Count the numbers and picture out each digit in your mind as you do so... Do your best to try and slow down the counting... This will slow down your breathing... In turn, it will also slow down your heartbeat...

Breathe in... 1... 2... 3... 4...

Hold... 1... 2... 3... 4...

And then release... 1... 2... 3... 4...

Now feel your heart's pace slowing down... As you concentrated on your breathing, it allowed your heart to slow things down... And with your heart beating at a more measured pace, it has also allowed your mind to decompress...

Breathe in... 1... 2... 3... 4...

Hold... 1... 2... 3... 4...

And then release... 1... 2... 3... 4...

Feel the panic start to subside... It starts to dissipate as your mind starts to regain its control... Your mind is also sending out a message to the rest of your body... Your mind tells your body that it is back in control...

Now feel the tensions you earlier felt ease up a bit. Feel some of the burden that weighed you down earlier lift... The fear is still there but the panic is gone...

The best thing you can realize at this point is that you are back in control... Panic is no longer holding you down... It does not bind you... It has released its grasp... You are free to take control... Take back the control...

Breathe in... 1... 2... 3... 4...

Hold... 1... 2... 3... 4...

And then release... 1... 2... 3... 4...

All it takes is to take back control of your breathing... This is how you fight back the panic attack... This is how you gain back control of yourself... All you have to do is to be in the here and now... Panic cannot touch you in the here and now... In the here and now, you can move, you can take action... you are in control...

Breathe in... 1... 2... 3... 4...

Hold... 1... 2... 3... 4...

And then release... 1... 2... 3... 4...

Now open your eyes and do what you have to do... You are now back in control...

DAY 8—DEEP RELAXATION [15 MINUTES]

Today marks the second week of your guided meditation for mindfulness journey. Congratulations for committing seven straight days of practicing mindfulness. The exercise today will focus on bringing you deep relaxation. This type of relaxation is perfect to end a busy day. The great thing about this exercise is that the duration is not that long. In fact, deep relaxation can be achieved in just 15 minutes.

To start, go back to your sweet spot. You should have established for yourself a place or venue where you can do your mindfulness exercises. Go to this place and settle in—start to feel comfortable. You may change into more comfortable clothing as this may help you breathe better.

Dim the lights and close the door and the windows. You want to ensure peace and quiet for this exercise. Close your eyes as you become more comfortable in your position. And then you can begin.

Start by focusing on your breath...

Breathe in... Hold... And then release...

Imagine the air that you are breathing... Try your best to imagine the air... Like it is visible... And you can see it enter your nose... You can see it fill your lungs... You can also see it exit out of you... Focus your thoughts on this and this alone... Relegate your other thoughts... Bring these unnecessary thoughts to the background... On the foreground of your mind is the air that you breathe...

Breathe in... Hold... And then release...

Be in the here and now... Let your cares and worries drift away... They leave you knowing that they don't matter in the here and now...

Breathe in... Hold... And then release...

Picture out your whole body... Try to imagine the whole of your present in your mind's eye... See your body as it is now... How are you now? How does your body feel?

As you gain awareness of your body, try to imagine your breath bring in relaxation to it... Every breath you take allows you to absorb relaxation... It settles inside of you as it disperses all throughout your body... And then as you exhale, all your cares and worries go with it... The tension and tightness that you felt a while ago are starting to also disappear...

Now feel your muscles relax... They become soft, like putty... Slowly but surely you are drifting into a more relaxed state... You can sense the lightness overcome you... Now you feel like you are floating on air... weightless... Nothing is holding you down... You feel delighted as you take in the experience...

And now your head is feeling light as well... You can feel all the cares and worries start to drift away... These errant thoughts are being replaced by thoughts of calmness and peace... of relaxation and stillness... of lightness... of weightlessness... of delight and bliss...

Breathe in... Hold... And then release...

Appreciate the feeling of deep relaxation... This is how it feels to be relaxed... This is how it feels to when your cares and worries are nowhere to be found... This is how it feels to be in the here and now...

Take another long and deep breath... Continue to be very intentional in your breathing... Bring in great desire as you execute each of your breaths...

Breathe in... Hold... And then release...

As you continue your breathing with great desire, realize that as your mind and body relax, your spirit relaxes as well... Imagine a light that glows within you... It has grown dim as it burned most of its energy trying to combat your tiredness and anxieties... But imagine this light now... It glows just a little brighter... It shines brighter as you breathe in and breathe out...

This is your soul... And it is recharging... As your body and mind relax, your soul is also regenerating... Continue with your breathing... Let the rhythm of your breathing increase the energy of your light within... Feel your body respond... Your body is getting more and more relaxed...

Remain in the here and now... It's time to bring yourself back... Bring in another burst of air...

Breathe in... Hold... And then release...

You have just undergone a relaxation experience so deep... You are refreshed... Bring awareness back to your body... Make slow movements to signal your intent to come back... And then you can open your eyes... Take another deep breath and then you can continue with your day... May you enjoy the remainder of your day and have a good night's sleep later...

DAY 9—SUNSET MINDFULNESS [15 MINUTES]

The sunset has a restorative and healing power. You can certainly feel its effects and power if you take the time to see and experience its beauty. Let the power of the sunset bring you closer to mindfulness with this exercise. All this exercise requires from you is for you to sit back, relax, and enjoy the beauty of the sun as it calls it day.

You need to be outdoors for this exercise. Try to find a nice and quiet spot outside. Make sure this place is devoid of people—you want to enjoy only your own presence for this exercise. So settle down in this place and get comfortable. There will be no need to close your eyes for this exercise. You need them opened so that you will be able to enjoy the full majesty of the sunset. Time your exercise as the sun is about to set. This should take about fifteen minutes so make sure you can be at your spot fifteen minutes before the sun sets.

Start by bringing your awareness to your breathing…

Breathe in… Hold… And then release…

Breathe in the late afternoon air… Let it introduce calmness within you… The day is about to end… There's no more need to rush… Life is starting to slow its pace once again… Let your mind and body move at the world's current pace… It is back to normal speed… It is back in the here and now…

Be in the here and now... And in this afternoon you find yourself perched on your sweet spot ready to take in the majesty and brilliance of the sun as it sets...

Be in the here and now... Just like the sun... The sun is always in the here and now... In the here and now, the sun understands its place, understands about the passing of time... Its place is as steady as it has always been... Its time is ever constant, ever running... Know that it is us who move... We are forever in motion... And it seems to us that it is the sun that is moving... But it's an illusion...

The sun has always been in the here and now... It stays in place and always acknowledges the time... We need to be in the same place and time as the sun... To be in the here and now...

Breathe in... Hold... And then release...

Our now is the experiencing of the sunset... It is one of nature's gifts to mankind... It is as constant as time... It is forever there, because as long as the sun rises in the east, it will surely set in the west... That is the message of the sun to us... And it is up to us to behold its beauty and wisdom...

For the sun is in the here and now... We, too, can be in the here and now... Just like the sun...

Behold the sun as is slowly moves down... down to the horizon... Behold the soft hues and the gentle light that the sunset brings... Notice the beauty of everything the light touches... The light of the sunset brings out the soft colors of the world around you... Appreciate the softness... Appreciate the beauty... This is the sun's gift to you...

Breathe in... Hold... And then release...

See the clouds in their striking colors... See the yellows, reds, and oranges... Notice the hints of blue fading... The fiery colors are invading the sky... Try to see if you can spot hints of purples and pinks on the sky... See the whole sky and all its beauty... The sky is like a painter's masterpiece... It is like a canvass that has been touched by the paintbrush of a master... This is the sun's gift to you...

Breathe in... Hold... And then release...

And so the sun settles on the horizon... It slowly descends until you can no longer see it... The sky is left radiating with the colors but it grows darker now... The sun has called it a day...

And you should also call it a day as well... It's time to wind down your activities... It's time for rest...

This is the here and now that you find yourself in... The here and now that calls for you to slow down and rest... Tomorrow will be another day full of activity... And you can be sure of that just as sure as the sun rises in the east...

Go on... Continue with the rest of your day at a slower pace... Rest and recharge... The sun has set...

DAY 10—AFTER WORK STRESS-RELIEVING MEDITATION [15 MINUTES]

So the workday is finally done and you can now start to kick back and relax. You had a full day and it was all about making sure you achieved your goals. For sure your day was full of physical and mental activities. These activities will take a toll on your mind and body. It is best to practice mindfulness and try to achieve some relaxation as you close out your day. This exercise is the perfect activity to gain that stress-relief as you end your busy day.

Make sure that all your tasks and activities are done before you start doing this exercise. Go to your sweet spot and settle in. You might want to have dinner first before doing this activity. And a warm shower will do you good as well. Once you're ready, settle down and get comfortable.

As always, bring your focus to your breathing…

Breathe in… Hold… And then release…

Start to get a sense of how your body is feeling right now… Feel the sensations of your body… Let these feelings manifest themselves…

Try to feel the tightness of some of your muscles… Can you identify these spots? What particular areas are feeling tight? These are probably the areas that did most of your activities… These must be the areas that brought you the success you achieved today... You can feel proud of these muscles... They served you well....

Next, try to feel the tiredness of your legs and feet... They brought you to places... They made sure you stood up... They held your weight... They are another reason for your success... Feel proud of your legs and feet... They served you well...

Now try to feel your back and shoulders... Maybe you can feel some aches and pains as you move... Your back has held you steady all throughout the day... Again, your back and shoulders are another reason why you got through your day just fine... You can feel proud of your back and shoulders... They served you well...

Lastly, feel your head... feel your mind... It must feel heavy after all the mental processing you did as you worked... Appreciate the power of your mind... This piece of bodily organ is making sure you are functioning well... And it brought you ideas and thoughts so crucial for your success... Feel proud of your mind... It served you well...

Breathe in... Hold... And then release...

Breathe in... Hold... And then release...

Breathe in... Hold... And then release...

Let your breathing bring forth relaxation... Let it bring you rest... Let it ease your overworked mind and overburdened body...

Each breath you take makes the tension that you are feeling go away... Your breathing is causing your muscles to relax... Imagine the air your take in reach your whole body... It untangles the knots in your muscles... It lets your muscles free... It lets them breathe...

Imagine also your head and mind feel freer with each breath that you take... Your breathing is freeing your mind from its worries... It also sweeps away the cobwebs and the dust that has started to accumulate in your mind... You can feel your head feel light...

Your back, shoulders, and neck also feel freer... They can respond much better to the movement now as you breathe in more relaxation... You can feel the tightness ease away with each breath you take...

Breathe in... Hold... And then release...

Remember that you are in the here and now... Your body is starting to rest in the here and now... Your body is starting to bring its energy back... Your body is recuperating...

And as you continue your slow and steady breathing, you can see stress escaping your body... Stress was the key component of your brilliant performance earlier in the day... You needed that stress in order for you to function at your peak...

But the day is about to end and all your activities are done... There's no need for the stress anymore... There's absolutely no need to hold on to them... So let them escape you... Maintain your breathing and continue to be in the here and now...

Breathe in... Hold... And then release...

In the here and now your stress is dissipating...

It's time to bring yourself back... Start by bringing more energy into your muscles... Start to move them slowly... And then open your eyes and stand up... You can get through the remainder of the day with your stress greatly reduced...

DAY 11—PAUSING FOR RELAXATION [15 MINUTES]

It's just nice to be able to pause sometimes. When the day gets too hectic, when life starts to move a little too fast, it is but appropriate to stop for a few moments. This will enable you to get your bearings back. You can reorient yourself and gain that little bit of extra energy needed for you to finish strong. This exercise will enable you to activate this pause. And hopefully, it will bring you the relaxation your need.

As you gain awareness that your day might be headed for a frantic finish, it's important to just stop... Just pause... Hold off whatever it was you were doing... Just stop and try to regain your balance...

Try to find a place where you can be alone... It would be hard to pause and meditate if there are so many people with you and around you... So go to this place... Excuse yourself... Tell the people you're with that you need just fifteen minutes... This is all you need to be able to pause and relax... And then you can continue and get on with your day...

As you settle into your spot, try and get comfortable... You might be feeling heavy sensations... You could be going through some anxieties... Don't worry, these things are normal... Feel free to acknowledge these feelings and anxieties... But do not dwell on them... Try to let them pass as you acknowledge them... Let them be on their way... You need to be able to relax first...

Get a hold of yourself and bring your focus to your breathing...

Breathe in... Hold... And then release...

Breathe in... Hold... And then release...

Breathe in... Hold... And then release...

Let your breathing slow down your body's motions... Let it slow down your heartbeat... As you gain more control in your breathing, you will find your heart rate start to slow down... You need this sensation so that you can feel that you are back in control...

And with this control back, bring yourself to the only place and time you need to be... In the here and now...

It is in the here and now that you can pause... It is in the here and now where you can stop and take stock of what's happening... It is in the here and now where you can let your mind and body rest for a little bit...

Breathe in... Hold... And then release...

In the here and now time starts to move a little slower... It moves in consonance with your heart... It moves to the rhythm of your beating heart... The more you slow your breathing down, the more it seems like time is creeping and crawling at a snail's pace...

Let this feeling bring your relaxation... Let it bring your calmness... This relaxation and calmness are what your body and mind need right now... Let the relaxation and calmness relieve you of your burdens, even if the relief is only temporary...

Breathe in… Hold… And then release…

Just be in the here and now… The here and now is you not doing anything… The here and now is what allows you to just stop… The absence of activity allows your mind to be at ease… It allows your mind to regroup…

By pausing you are bringing your control back… Stopping has allowed you to reclaim this control… You handed this control over to your cares and worries momentarily… But you retrieved it… You pried it from their clutches… Because they do not own control… You own it… You are in control…

So control whatever it is you can… And for those that you can't, let it go… Those are not in the here and now… What is in the here and now are the things that you can control…

Breathe in… Hold… And then release…

Now it's time to restart… You had your time to pause… You regained possession of your control… You can continue with your day… Your pause will enable you to finish your day strong…Take a deep breath and count backward…

Breathe in… 3…

Hold… 2…

And then release… 1…

Open your eyes and continue with your day…

DAY 12—THE ALERTNESS MEDITATION [15 MINUTES]

Wouldn't it be great to have a burst of alertness when you start to feel lethargic and listless? Well, it is possible. You can get a dose of alertness just by focusing your mind. Mindfulness can elevate your energy levels and bring you to a state of alertness. All it takes is for you to make time and a private place and you can be on your way to alertness. Try this exercise to bring out the alertness in you.

Excuse yourself and find a place where you won't be bothered. As you feel the thralls of lethargy and boredom, you need time for yourself to bring your energy levels back. So go find a private space. Settle down and get comfortable. Begin the exercise once you feel settled...

You can close your eyes to help ward off distractions... Start by focusing on your breathing... Imagine the air that surrounds you... Try to envision visible air... It is all around you... It swirls, dances, and floats...

Now imagine yourself bringing that air inside your body as you breathe... You can see the air traipse and dance as it makes its way into your nose... And then visualize the path it is taking as it enters your body... See with your mind's eye how it travels from your nostrils to your airways to your lungs... And as it enters your lungs it gives it power and energy... This is the same energy that is distributed all throughout your body... And then picture how the air behaves as it leaves your body...

Breathe in... Hold... And then release...

Your body and brain have grown listless... It has grown tired... Perhaps it got overwhelmed by too much information... Perhaps there was nothing that created a spark... Perhaps it is just tired... You can feel your attention and focus starting to decline...

But notice how your body and mind behaves as you breathe... Notice how they react when oxygen is introduced to them... They actually gain more energy with each breath that you take... Your body and mind need air... It needs the energy brought by the oxygen...

So get a hold of yourself... And get a hold of your breathing...

Breathe in... Hold... And then release...

Breathe in... Hold... And then release...

Breathe in... Hold... And then release...

Bring yourself in the here and now... The here and now is the only place and time that matters... The here and now will bring you to alertness...

Breathe in... Hold... And then release...

You can start to feel a slight spark start to emerge from within you...

Breathe in... Hold... And then release...

The spark starts to intensify... Slowly at first...

Breathe in... Hold... And then release...

It now becomes a fire that burns... You can feel the heat... You can feel the energy...

Breathe in... Hold... And then release...

This fire that burns from within gets bigger and bigger with each breath you take... Let it burn brighter...

Breathe in... Hold... And then release...

This fire is your alertness... This fire is your energy... It is alive once again... Your breathing jumpstarted it... Let your breathing bring forth your desired energy... Feel it surge once more... Your energy will bring with it alertness... And permit this alertness to bring you vigor as you go through your day's remaining activities...

Continue to be in the here and now... Let your breathing rhythm continue... Each breath brings with it the oxygen needed to enable the fire that burns within you burn brighter...

Breathe in... Hold... And then release...

You have regained your alertness... You can now go back and finish what you need to do... You now have the energy necessary to get through the day... Feel your alertness continue to rise as you take in each breath...

And now you are ready to get back... Maintain your breathing rhythm as you bring yourself back... Feel the energy surge... Let your body adjust to your surroundings... Move them a bit so that you can start to bring yourself back... And when you're ready, open your eyes... You should now be able to get back to your day feeling recharged and full of alertness...

DAY 13—CALMING AFTER A PANIC ATTACK [15 MINUTES]

When a panic attack grips you, you will usually find yourself unable to move. You will feel that you are paralyzed even though your body is still able to function. What's happening is that your brain becomes so overworked by the panic it feels that it will have a hard time commanding your body. That is why it is important that you regain your control as fast as you can. And you can only achieve that once you feel calmer. This meditative exercise can help you achieve that calmness.

You can start this activity the moment your panic attack starts to subside. As you gain a little composure, you can then decide to pause. You need to stop your activities. If you can, you also need to put a pause to whatever it was you were thinking.

This pause can be achieved by putting focus on your breathing. So close your eyes and bring your awareness to your breathing...

Breathe in... Hold... And then release...

It will do you well to be mindful of how you breathe... Bring in intentness with every breath.... Be deliberate as you allow the air to enter your body... Do it with such a desire that it brings newfound energy to your body... Focus on it... Experience it... Live it... Be aware of your breathing...

Breathe in… Hold… And then release…

And now bring yourself in the here and now… Know that this is the only place that matters… The fears that you experienced earlier, the cause of your panic, well, they do not exist in the here and now… It's either their existence has come to pass… These are your fears that happened in the past… Or these fears have yet to happen… Once again, they do not matter… Not here… Not now…

Breathe in… Hold… And then release…

The here and now is about you taking back control… The here and now is you being deliberate in your breathing… This is your way to bring control back… You know that this will enable you to be closer in the here and now…

Now allow calm to enter your body… Allow calm to enter your mind…

You have put your fears in their place… You have transported them to somewhere not in the here and now… That place is where they belong… They shouldn't hold residence in the here and now…

You can actually let calmness in now with your fears in their proper place….

Feel the calmness start to infiltrate your body… They can now start to penetrate your core… This calmness takes away the messy feelings you were feeling when you started to panic… This calmness is taking away the weight that pinned you down earlier… Allow the calmness to work its magic... Allow the calmness to transport you to another place... A place where you are in control...

Breathe in... Hold... And then release...

You gain more calmness the more you breathe... Steady your breathing... Let it follow its natural rhythm...

Feel the calmness flow down to your lower body... Feel it take the pressure off your feet and legs... You feel more nimble now that your lower body is unburdened...

Feel the calmness settle in your core... It enters at the seat of your soul... It brings you the warmth you needed... The warmth you lost earlier when you were panicking... The calmness brings you a sense of security... It emboldens you... It takes some of the doubt away...

And then feel the calmness do its wonders on your mind... You can now think clearer thoughts... The fear that blocked your thoughts earlier is gone... It is now replaced by the calmness that you feel... Your mind feels sharp... You can now focus... You feel so in control... This feeling brings back the confidence you lost earlier... It boosts your ego... Now you know you can get through with this challenge just fine... Because you are calm...

Breathe in... Hold... And then release...

Appreciate the steadiness that you feel now... Know that you can gain control of yourself once you let the calmness in... You can gain control of yourself as you bring yourself in the here and now...

Remain in the here and now...

Breathe in... Hold... And then release...

And now, feel free to bring yourself back... The panic attack you felt a while ago is not here anymore... It is now replaced by calmness... It is now replaced by steadiness... Feel that you are in control of yourself by moving your body... Know that your body follows your mind's every command... No need to dwell on your fear... You have placed that fear where it belongs... You can now stand up to that fear... You are confident enough to face it... And when you're ready, open your eyes... Welcome back!

DAY 14—EASY-TO-FOLLOW SELF-HEALING MEDITATION [20 MINUTES]

Your mind is very powerful. It is powerful enough to heal itself. And it is more than capable of healing your body. All you need to do is to divert your focus and point it straight into your self-healing capacity. Tap the power of your mind so that it can do the process of convalescence. This meditation exercise is the clincher for your second week of practice. As such, you will continue by focusing on mindfulness as you try to achieve relaxation. But the ultimate goal for this exercise will be self-healing. And through this exercise, it can be done in an easy-to-follow method.

Start the exercise as you did in the other relaxation exercises—go to your comfortable place. Situate yourself in a position that will bring you relaxation and calmness. You can wear loose clothing so that your body can be well-ventilated and can breathe better. Dim the lights of your room and focus on intensifying your relaxation. You can start by closing your eyes.

As always, bring your attention to your breathing. Put in all your effort and attention to how you breathe... Let all your desire flow with the air that you take in... Be intentional as you go about it.... Be deliberate... Do it purposefully... Be one with it...

Breathe in... Hold... And then release...

Visualize the air that you breathe... See it in your mind's eye... Trace its journey from the outside of your body to the inside... Visualize how it travels from your nose to your lungs... Imagine the air reaching your core... Imagine it giving you life... Imagine it allowing your cells to burn energy... And then continue to trace its journey... This time as it makes its way out of you... Imagine the air sweeping with it all the impurities in your body along with it as it exits you...

You are breathing in relaxation and energy... You are expelling your body's impurities as you exhale... Let the goodness in... And let the tension and tightness out...

Breathe in... Hold... And then release...

Try to remember your goal... Try to remember how it is to be mindful... Just be in the here and now... The here and now is the only place and time you need to be in...

Be in the here and now as you focus on your breathing... Be in the here and now as you visualize taking more and more relaxation from the air around you... Be in the here and now as you imagine all the impurities being expelled from your body as you exhale...

Breathe in... Hold... And then release...

Breathe in... Hold... And then release...

Breathe in... Hold... And then release...

Now try to feel your whole body... Feel where it hurts... Feel your ailments... Feel the parts of your body that are not well... Go ahead and take your time... You are in no hurry... Just feel... Let the pain and discomfort reach you... Just feel these conditions that are in you...

And then feel the sensations that these pain and discomfort bring with them... What other feelings do they give you? Try to feel all of them... Put them together with the ailments... Let them take part in this exercise... Go ahead... Just feel them... Take your time...

Breathe in... Hold... And then release...

Breathe in... Hold... And then release...

Breathe in... Hold... And then release...

Remember that you are in the here and now... And in the here and now you feel some discomfort... You also feel pain... You feel some sort of sickness... Your head is heavy... Your body is languid... Your muscles feel tired... Your whole body is in disarray... Go ahead and feel these sensations... It's perfectly normal to feel these... These are the symptoms of an unwell body...

Now it's time for you to heal yourself...

Imagine a bright light shining on top of your head... This bright light starts out as a small ball at first... And then it grows bigger... And it gets brighter still... Its radiance intensifies... And you can now feel its warmth...

This is the healing light... This is the light that will enable your body to recover... This is the light that will ease all discomfort... This is the light that will try to take away the pain...

Let this light enter you... Allow its radiance to shine upon you... Starting from your head, down to your toes... Let the light cover you completely... Let its luminescence pierce through your skin... Give consent to it... And let it do its wonderful work on you... Let the healing light start your self-healing process...

Breathe in... Hold... And then release...

The power of the healing light makes you feel all warm inside... You feel a delightful sensation as it swathes your whole body with healing energy... You are starting to feel more relaxed... The light is bringing you to a whole new level of calmness... It makes you feel very comfortable... very still...

And pretty soon you start to notice your body responding to the healing energy of the light... You start to feel very light... Your muscles do not harbor the tightness it felt earlier... Your head is free from the burden that troubled it a while ago... Your whole body is glowing with the energy of the light... You are starting to heal... Feel the healing process... Feel the discomfort and pain start to subside...

Breathe in... Hold... And then release...

You are bringing in more relaxation as you breathe... And you are expelling pain and discomfort more and more...

And you are still in the here and now... In the here and now you are healing... Your body is regenerating... It is restoring itself... So that you can function better... So that you can have more freedom... So that you can live your life unhampered... So that you can stay longer in the here and now...

Let your thoughts remain with the light... It covers you with such brightness that you can feel a tingling vibration from within... This is the power of the healing light...

And then it's time for the light to go... It slowly leaves you... But the healing process continues... Stay with the feeling of healing...

Breathe in... Hold... And then release...

Reacquaint yourself with your surroundings... Try to move your body a bit... Stretch your muscles so that you can feel the energy recirculate... And then open your eyes... You have just undergone self-healing...

DAY 15—SELF-CONFIDENCE MEDITATION [20 MINUTES]

A lack of self-confidence can hamper your performance big time. Sometimes, doing well is just a matter of having the right levels of confidence. You can do great things if you believe in yourself. But confidence can prove to be elusive at times. What do you do if your supply of self-confidence seems to be in short supply? You can dig deep within you and let your mind manufacture it. That's right, you can will yourself to be more confident. And you can do it through a mindfulness meditation exercise.

For this exercise, you need to be in a place where you can be alone. This place should preferably have a mirror. It is best to do this exercise before you attempt at a pressure-packed performance. Or you can do this regularly as you retire for the night.

Start by facing yourself in the mirror. You may stand for this exercise. Standing will give your body more energy. And more energy means more confidence. But feel free to be seated if you wish. Look at your reflection straight in the eye...

And then you can start focusing on your breathing...

Breathe in... Hold... And then release...

Maintain eye contact with the person you see in the mirror while you breathe...

Notice the contours of the face of the person in the mirror... Try to see the shapes and forms that you can see before you... See the person in front of you reflect your every action... Bring the person you see in the mirror in the here and now...

Breathe in... Hold... And then release...

Remember that the only place and time that matters is the here and now... Doubt and regret have no place in the here and now... In the here and now, it's just you... Just you and the person you see in the mirror... That person is also you... And you can feed the person you see in the mirror with confidence...

Visualize the air around you... See with your mind's eye this air that surrounds every inch of the room you are in... Know that the air around you has energy... And this energy is what you need in order to bring in confidence within you...

You need to take in this energy in the air...

Breathe in...

Hold... Let the energy intensify as you hold your breath...

And as you release your breath, blow it to the person in the mirror... Let the person in the mirror receive the energy from your breath... This is the energy that will give the person you see in the mirror confidence... Observe your reflection doing the same... The person in the mirror is also blowing energized air to you... Receive this air... Receive the energy... Feel your confidence rise...

Feel yourself soar higher as you take in more and more energy... You have received a much-needed boost in confidence...

Continue to blow the air to your reflection...

Breathe in... Hold... And then release...

Breathe in... Hold... And then release...

Breathe in... Hold... And then release...

Now say to yourself, "I am confident!"

Say, "I can overcome this. I know I can do this. I will do this... I'm doing this now."

Say, "I have what it takes to succeed."

Feel your energy rise as you say each word... Feel your confidence reach a higher level with each utterance...

And now it's time for you to visualize success... Visualize how your victory will look like... You may close your eyes for this... Play it out in your mind... Picture yourself executing and performing with great confidence... Picture yourself performing your best... Picture yourself at your peak... Let this picture stay with you... Let it be etched in your mind...

Be in the here and now... You are focusing on increasing your confidence... You are visualizing success and victory... You have put doubt and regret to the side where they cannot bother you... Because doubt and regret have no place in the here and now....

Breathe in... Hold... And then release...

Now it's time to open your eyes... Time to take a look at your reflection again... See the person in the mirror... And see the difference... Notice how the eyes of the person in the mirror sparkle with confidence... Notice the smile starting to form on the face... It's a smile of self-assurance... But this self-assurance does not border on overconfidence... It is just enough to lift the spirits of anyone who sees it...

Appreciate the spirit of the person you see in front of you... See the aura of the person in the mirror... It burns brighter... You can no longer sense doubt... All you can see and feel is confidence... Appreciate the beauty of the person in front of you... Appreciate how confidence can bring the best out of that person...

And then realize that the person you see in the mirror is you... The confidence that you can sense is the confidence that is inside of you... You upped your self-confidence as you heightened the energy you got from within...

Breathe in... Hold... And then release...

Now it's time to conclude this exercise... Take in another long and deep breath...

Breathe in... Inhale the energy that's in the air...

Hold... Let the energy intensify as you hold your breath...

And as you release your breath, blow it to the person in the mirror... Give your reflection energy one last time...

Take a good look at yourself and then move away from the mirror... Continue to feel your confidence soar... Feel the wonderful feeling of increasing your energy and your confidence... You may stand up... And as you do, continue to let your energy and confidence increase... Then go about the rest of your day with great confidence...

DAY 16—THANKFULNESS AFTER A FULL DAY [20 MINUTES]

Your day will end on a high note if you choose to cap it off in high spirits. A thankful heart will always lighten the mood. This thankfulness will enable you to see all the good that has happened within your day. This will allow you to see that the glass is indeed half full. So end your day with a thankfulness meditation. This exercise will teach you how to be aware and how to be mindful of all the good things that happened to you.

This exercise is one of the lighter exercises in this book, if not the lightest. You can do this anywhere. You can even do this while walking. All you need for this exercise is a time and place. That's all you need for you to be in the here and now…

Start with your breathing… Put your focus on it… Desire every breath you take… And then be forceful as you release that breath…

Breathe in… Hold… And then release…

Just go with the flow of your breathing… Follow its rhythm… Become aware of it… Let your breathing sing a happy duet with your heart beat…

Breathe in… Hold… And then release…

And as you release your exhalation, exclaim a silent "thank you"…

Feel the lightness of your heart as you do it... Feel your heart flutter as you utter the silent word of thanks... Feel your heart fill with gratitude... And let this gratitude bring in joy... Let it also bring you great satisfaction...

Once again...

Breathe in... Hold... And then release...

And don't forget to say another thank you... You can't utter thank you enough... Feel free to say it over and over again... In fact, say it again now... Say, "thank you"....

This is your heart speaking... This is your heart telling the world how much it appreciates being alive... How much it appreciates being able to take in the sweet air... And that's why you exclaim a thank you with each breath... Let each moment be a moment of joy... Be grateful for this... Be grateful for your existence... Let your existence remain in the here and now...

Think of all the wonderful things that happened today... Think of all the joyous occasions that transpired... Think of everything that made you smile... These are the things that made you enjoy your day... Be thankful that these occasions became part of your life today...

Now think of the not-so-happy happenings... Think of the hurt and the pain... Think of the ugly and the disastrous things that happened... Feel them weigh you down... But let them quickly pass... The reason why you're feeling them now is that you also want to be thankful for them... Be thankful because they are still a part of your life... Life is not worth living with these happenings... You take the good with the bad... For how can you appreciate the good things in life without the bad things? Be thankful still... These are the happenings that remind you that you're human after all...

Breathe in... Hold... And then release...

Breathe in... Hold... And then release...

And now think of the people that are close to you... These are the people that matter most to you... These are the people you care about... These are the people you love... Try to see each of their faces in your mind's eye... Let their image stay with you for a few moments... Try to feel their presence even if they're not there with you...

Go ahead, take your time in thinking about these people... After all, these are the people you love... These are your friends, colleagues, neighbors, family, children, partner, lover... These are the people that make you who you are... These people helped shape you... These people are also the reason why you continue to strive and do your best in this world...

Think of these people and say their names under your breath... Go ahead and name them one by one... And as you do so, say a word of thanks to them... Thank them for making your life the way it is... Thank them for making a huge impact on your life... Just thank them... For being there for you when you need them...

Breathe in... Hold... And then release...

Breathe in... Hold... And then release...

Remember to be in the here and now... Know that your heart is thankful and feels light when it is in the here and now...

Notice your surroundings now... Notice the passage of time... Concentrate on your breathing and the lightness of your heart... Stay with this feeling and let it fill your whole being... Continue to be in the spirit of gratitude... Continue to be thankful... And be in the here and now... Be thankful that you are in the here and now...

Now turn your attention to the day as it ends... The end of the day is drawing near... And you were able to live your life and do your work earlier... And as the day ends, it promises a tomorrow... This tomorrow is its assurance of a new beginning... And a new beginning is provided for you every single day... Be thankful for this... Feel the gratitude well up... Feel the gratitude grow on you...

You can look forward to a new day tomorrow... For tonight, it's just a matter of closing this chapter... And this exercise you are doing now—being thankful—is a wonderful nightcap for you to end another great day...

Breathe in... Hold... And then release...

Breathe in... Hold... And then release...

Breathe in... Hold... And then release...

As you exhale, say, "Thank you."

This time, make your voice louder... Make sure the world can hear you...

In a clear and audible voice, say, "Thank you."

So this ends your thankfulness meditation... Feel free to continue and you can start doing something else... Keep the spirit of gratitude burning within you... This is the spirit that makes everything light... This ends your gratitude meditation exercise...

DAY 17—DEALING WITH HEAVY EMOTIONS [20 MINUTES]

Sometimes you might feel that there are things holding you down. You might not be able to put a finger on these things—you just feel them. They're weighing heavy in your heart. Most likely, these things weighing your down are emotions. These emotions might be remnants of past or present hurts. Through meditative practice, you can enable yourself to place these emotions where they belong. Doing so might allow you the chance to move forward with your life.

Go to your comfortable spot for this exercise... You might want to lie down as things might get heavy as this exercise progresses... Wear loose and comfortable clothing... And make sure that there is nothing that can hamper your breathing...

When you're ready, you can start by closing your eyes... Try to focus on your breathing... Breathe with intentionality... Breathe with desire... Bring your whole being with you as you breathe... Focus on it and try to block out everything else, if you can... Really pour all your attention on your breathing...

Breathe in... Hold... And then release...

Breathe in... Hold... And then release...

Breathe in... Hold... And then release...

Feel your body start to relax as you put more awareness on your breathing... You can sense the rhythm of your breathing... It jives with the beating of your heart... Their motions bring another form of awareness to you... It lets you realize that you are in the here and now...

Let your body take in the relaxation... Allow this feeling to soften your stiff muscles... Allow it to unclench your fists... Allow it to unfurrow your brows... Let it ease your worries... Let it wipe away all errant thoughts...

Breathe in... Hold... And then release...

Breathe in... Hold... And then release...

Breathe in... Hold... And then release...

At this point, try to revisit the heaviness that you were feeling earlier... Is this heaviness felt in your head? Or is it prominent in your heart? Try to feel it... Try to relive the sensations... Try to bring them back... Allow it... It's the only way... As you allow them to return, you further your chances of moving on...

So let them overtake you once again... Let the heavy feelings overcome you... And feel free to let the emotions flow...

You may shed tears... cry... It's only natural...

You can shout in anger... You can bang your fist...

Go ahead and utter those curses... Feel the rage...

Or feel the frustration... Or is it guilt that you feel? Probably it's regret...

Go ahead and feel these emotions... Take your time to internalize everything... Let their weight fall on you... Let the heaviness of these emotions trample you once again...

Breathe in... Hold... And then release...

Breathe in... Hold... And then release...

Breathe in... Hold... And then release...

Bring yourself back to the here and now... Set aside those emotions for a moment... Let them stand still... Bring them to a corner and let them remain there... Know that they are not going anywhere... For this moment, this is where they will stay...

Breathe in... Hold... And then release...

Breathe in... Hold... And then release...

You are back in the here and now... In the here and now, there are no heavy feelings... In the here and now you simply exist... You are just you... to be how you should be... There are no heavy feelings in the here and now...

Get ready to go back to where you placed your heavy emotions... Prepare yourself to let go of them...

Approach the place where you left your heavy emotions... Do this slowly... Be intentional in your approach... Bring in desire with each step you take...

Breathe in... Hold... And then release...

Get ready to let go of your heavy emotions...

It's time for you to heal... It's time for you to forgive... To forgive those that hurt you... And to forgive also yourself... This is how you move on... This is how you can be rid of the weight that was pinning you down...

Imagine a body of water before you... This is the body of water where you will cast away your heavy emotions... The water will take them away... They will float away from you... Until they reach a very far place... Until they are at a safe distance... So far away that they will no longer bother you...

But first, you need to cut the cord that binds you with these emotions... Cut the string with your hand... The string is not tough to cut... Even a weak effort can cut it... So go ahead and cut... Cut away at all strings that attach you to these emotions... Break free from them...

And then cast them off to the water... One by one... Throw them to the body of water... See in your mind's eye the way you throw away these emotions... And now see the way they start to float away... They are gaining distance... And soon they are gone... Also gone are the strings that attached you to them... You can no longer feel their pull... Their weight is off your shoulders... You are free...

It's time for you to enjoy your freedom... Feel the lightness of your being now... This is how it feels when you are rid of the heavy emotions... You feel relaxed...

You feel calm... You feel a certain stillness... You feel peace...

Breathe in... Hold... And then release...

Breathe in... Hold... And then release...

Breathe in... Hold... And then release...

Remain in the here and now... You have achieved your freedom... This is what the here and now gives to you... Be free in the here and now...

It's time for you to return to where you were when you started the exercise... At this point, you can start to wiggle your fingers and toes so that you can bring yourself back slowly... Enjoy the sensation of lightness that you are continuing to feel... Let your whole body delight in the pleasure... And when you're ready, open your eyes... You are now back...

DAY 18—THE DARKNESS AND INTO NOTHINGNESS [20 MINUTES]

You appreciated life and everything that comes with it in one of the earlier exercises. For this exercise, you will come to appreciate the opposite. You will come to appreciate nothingness as you focus on the darkness. For you to appreciate life's activities, you need to learn to appreciate the nothingness that comes with it. Take this journey into the darkness. You can come out with a better appreciation and understanding of life as you take the plunge into the darkness.

Find your comfortable spot once again. Settle down and try to achieve a position that is both natural and relaxing. Make sure that your position is not putting any strain on your body. Try to relax your muscles. Feel free to recline for this activity. And more importantly, make sure that all lights are off. You may want to wear a blindfold to enhance the experience.

When you are ready, you can begin your journey into darkness...

Focus on your breathing...

Breathe in... Hold... And then release...

Breathe in... Hold... And then release...

Breathe in... Hold... And then release...

Know that in the darkness, the only thing that matters is your breathing... Because it is your breathing that will bring you to the most important place and time... This place and time is where you need to be right now... You want to be in the here and now... Be in the here and now...

Breathe in... Hold... And then release...

You see nothing... Everything is dark... Let this sink in... Try to orient yourself as you take this mindfulness journey in total darkness...

In the dark, you cannot see anything... In terms of sight, there is nothing...

How does this make you feel? What sensations are brought by the darkness? Does the darkness activate your fear response just like when you were a child? Don't worry, you are in a safe place... You were always in a safe place... You're just in the here and now... And in this here and now, there's just an absence of light...

Focus on your breathing once again... Don't lose your intention and desire as you breathe...

Breathe in... Hold... And then release...

Listen to your self breathe in total darkness... Listen to the sound you make as you inhale... And as you exhale... There's a certain rhythm to it... Listen and train your ears to this rhythm... And then listen to your heart... It beats at a measured pace... Its beating coincides with your breathing... It's like they're making music... Listen to this music... Focus only on this music until you won't be able to hear anything else... Focus so that the only thing you hear is the sound coming from your breathing and your heart... Try to achieve this nothingness in total darkness...

Breathe in... Hold... And then release...

Now start to notice the sensations that are starting to present themselves in the darkness... What do you feel in the dark? Or one way to ask this is: How do you feel? Try to find the words for each sensation that you're feeling... And then just feel these sensations...

And go back to your breathing...

Breathe in... Hold... And then release...

Let each breath take away the sensations... Let each inhalation and exhalation dull your senses... It's time to let these feelings flow out of you... Allow them to leave you... Just be in the here and now...

In the here and now, you feel nothing and you see nothing... You are shrouded by darkness... This darkness also takes away the sensations... And you can hear close to nothing... The only sounds that remain are the sounds of your breathing and the sound of your heart beating...

You are experiencing nothingness... This is the experience of the nothing... Because in the here and now you are nothing...

In the here and now you exist but you are also nothing... Let your mind process the irony... This is part of the paradox of existence... in order to be, you have to be nothing first... This is where you find yourself now... This is where you start... And nothingness is where you most likely will end...

Breathe in... Hold... And then release...

Breathe in... Hold... And then release...

Breathe in... Hold... And then release...

Just continue to drift in the nothingness... Continue to be in the darkness... There is no destination... There is no sense of counting time... Do not exert any effort... Cease all deliberate acts and thoughts... There is no desire present in the state of nothingness that you find yourself in...

You float aimlessly in this nothingness... And it's perfectly alright... You don't feel any pressure... The nothingness requires nothing from you... You just need to be... You just need to exist... Exist in the nothingness— this is another paradox... You just need to be in there here and now...

Unfortunately, the nothingness that you experienced is only temporary... It is but a teaser of the ultimate nothingness that will come... Relish the thought that you were able to experience momentary nothingness... Not a lot of people can do this... And you achieved it by putting yourself in the dark...

Breathe in... Hold... And then release...

You are starting to feel something already... But your world is still dark... Allow the feelings to come back... You are already veering away from the nothingness you felt earlier... Don't worry, you will come to settle to the usual activities of life pretty soon... Soon, you will start to experience everything...

Bring awareness back to your breathing... As you hear your breath and heartbeat, try to make out the sounds that are in your periphery... As you train your ears to listen, try to also feel the sensations coming back...

Once you are ready to return you can start to open your eyes in the dark... Your eyes will start to adjust to the darkness... And pretty soon you will start to distinguish the silhouettes of the things that surround you... As you can start to see in the dark, it's time for you to get up... You may turn on the light... And you can then start to feel everything... Everything is back as it was... Everything is now ready for you to experience it once again... Try to appreciate everything a little bit more...

DAY 19—FLOATING ON WATER [20 MINUTES]

The feeling of floating on water has a restorative and relaxing effect on the body and mind. There's just something about feeling weightless that makes you feel whole again. This is the reason why several therapeutic methods are incorporating the use of water. For this exercise, you will feel the effects of how it is to be floating on water. It will be relaxing and refreshing at the same time.

For this exercise, it is best if you do this in your bathtub. You can time this exercise while you are having a dip in the tub. Or another option is to do this while swimming in a pool or at the beach. If you don't have a bathtub and if a pool or beach is out of the question, you can just imagine being immersed in water.

Get started by immersing yourself in the water. Make sure that you can lie down in the water and that you can breathe just fine. Your breathing should be unhampered when doing this exercise. Acclimatize yourself with the water. Feel your body temperature adjust itself to the temperature of the water. Start to relax your whole body. Allow your muscles to soften as they are immersed in the water. And then close your eyes…

Begin by focusing your attention on your breathing…

Breathe in… Hold… And then release…

Focus on how your body is allowing oxygen to enter it... Visualize the process in your mind... And then feel the effects as the oxygen enters your body... Feel the oxygen distributed to your bloodstream... Experience the energy it brings... Feel alive with each breath you take...

Be in the here and now... Know that you are in a safe place... The here and now is the only place and time that matters...

Try to set aside the events of the day... These events are done... They are over... They are already part of your history... Set them aside and focus on the here and now...

Do your best to ward off those errant thoughts... Those are thoughts of yesterday... Or those are thoughts of tomorrow... Maybe those are thoughts of a while ago... Or thoughts of later... These thoughts have ceased to matter or have yet to matter... They are not in the here and now...

All you need is to be in the here and now...

Breathe in... Hold... And then release...

Breathe in... Hold... And then release...

Breathe in... Hold... And then release...

Notice what is going on around you... You are surrounded by water... Imagine you are floating... Imagine that you are weightless... All your weight is being supported by the water... Its buoyancy is pushing you to the surface...

You are safe in the water... The water will not let you drown... It does its best to keep you afloat... It will simply let you be...

It even comforts you, this water... As you float, the water rocks you back and forth... It also cradles you... You are like a baby floating on this water... A baby that is rocked to sleep... The water lulls your senses... It soothes and relaxes you as it cradles you... The gentle swaying of left to right, right to left makes you feel heavenly... You start to drift into nothingness as the water rocks you to calmness and relaxation... This nothingness is the here and now...

Be in the here and now...

Breathe in... Hold... And then release...

Take all the sensations that come with the experience of floating on water... Feel the water touch you... Feel it play around you... It splashes as you make even the tiniest of movements...

You feel the water rejuvenate your tired body... It reaches all the way to your pores... It gives your skin a gentle teasing touch... And each touch brings with it a form of energy that helps you recuperate...

You now feel your energy soar... This is the effect the water has on you... It has restored you... And not only your body, but your mind as well... The coolness of the air is coupled by the warmness of the water soothes both your mind and your soul...

Now you are one with the water... You can feel your body being incorporated into the water... Your whole body is now feeling very relaxed... It just goes with the flow of things... It simply exists... It has no worries or cares... Because water knows not these things... Water is simply water... It flows and takes the shape of its container... That is the nature of water... And that is how you feel now... Let this feeling take over you... Let the feeling of being one with the water overcome you... You are one with it and you are in the here and now...

Breathe in... Hold... And then release...

Feel the gentleness of water as you imagine yourself transformed into a liquid state... It is cool... It refreshes... It is soothing... But also know of water's potential for great power... This is the magnificence of water... It brings life... It refreshes... It soothes and cools... And yet it can be a source of power... It can be a source of greatness... And think of its abundance... Water is everywhere... The world is full of it... Even parts of your body are made up of water...

Continue to float... Continue to feel the calmness as you drift along... Know that you do not need any direction... You have no aim, no purpose... You simply need to be... To be in the here and now... You achieve this as you float... Continue to float... Be one with the water...

Breathe in... Hold... And then release...

Breathe in... Hold... And then release...

Breathe in... Hold... And then release...

And now it's time to come back... Time to end your floating in water... Bring yourself back gently... Start to let your senses come back... Re-acclimatize yourself to your surroundings... Continue to feel the water surrounding your body... Move your body just a little bit... You should be making small splashes as you do this... Feel and hear these splashes that you are making... And when you're ready, open your eyes...

DAY 20—THE CANDLE MEDITATION EXERCISE [25 MINUTES]

A candle meditation exercise is one of the most calming exercises in this book. What sets this exercise apart is that your focus and attention is diverted to something in front of you—the candle. It is easier to let go of your thoughts as you pour your focus and attention towards the candle. With the physical presence of the candle and the light of the fire, this exercise will let you reach a deeper level of mindfulness. Practicing the candle meditation exercise is one sure-fire way to improve your concentration.

There's a bit of preparation needed as you start this exercise. Prepare the room you will be in. And then also prepare a candle and something to light the candle with. Take a few minutes to prepare the whole space before you light the candle. Distribute your good energy all over the space. Shower it with your presence. Turn off the lights (or you can just turn them down). This exercise is much easier to do in the dark. Too much light in the room will dampen the mood.

Light the candle and settle down. Feel comfortable as you settle in your position. The best position for this exercise is sitting down and having the light of the candle at eye level. You may position your head a little lower if you wish. Just make sure that your head is not settled at a weird angle. Also make sure that your back is not slumping.

Feel the relaxation overtake all the other sensations... Settle in and get even more comfortable... Look at the light of the candle... Let the light contrast with the darkness of the room... Try to also be aware of your periphery... This is the darkness that surrounds you... And in front of you is a light source... The candle...

Continue by bringing your attention to your breathing... Put in your whole self as you breathe... Inhale and exhale with desire and intentness...

Breathe in... Hold... And then release...

Maintain your contact with the candle as you breathe... Connect with the light... See the light of the candle with intentness and desire... Continue to breathe naturally as you do this... Focus on the light... while you maintain the rhythm of your breathing...

Breathe in... Hold... And then release...

Breathe in... Hold... And then release...

Breathe in... Hold... And then release...

You are in the here and now... In the here and now it is dark... Darkness covers the room you are in... But in the here and now there is light in front of you... The light is small but it illuminates the room... It fills the room with its presence...

As such, this light also fills you with its presence... It is small... It's just a flicker in the vastness of the place you are in... But it is enough to bring you some awareness of the room you are in... It is enough to bring your awareness to the here and now...

Breathe in... Hold... And then release...

Breathe in... Hold... And then release...

Breathe in... Hold... And then release...

See the fire on the wick of the candle... See the motion it does... You can see it dancing... As if it has a life of its own... As if it has motivation from within... Wanting you to watch it... So it dances... It flickers... It sways back and forth... But it never leaves the wick of the candle...

You can start to feel a little bit of heat... This is the heat coming from the fire of the candle... This heat is just enough for you to distinguish it in the coldness of the room... You feel its warmth... It is a welcome feeling... You let this warmth enrich you... You let the sensations flow to your body... You relish it... It's a wonderful feeling to feel the warmth of the candle...

Breathe in... Hold... And then release...

Breathe in... Hold... And then release...

Imagine that each breath brings life to the fire... Imagine it is your breathing that is powering the fire of the candle... You can actually see the fire dance more furtively as you inhale and exhale... This is your capacity to give life to others... Like your breath on the candle, your spirit is capable of touching others in ways that will motivate and inspire them... Continue to give life to the candle... Breathe with intent and desire... And then absorb the energies of the candle as you breathe... It also gives you spirit... It makes you feel alive... Let the candle help you experience the here and now...

Be in the here and now... Focus on the candle... In the here and now, all you have is the darkness around you and the light of the candle in front of you...

Breathe in... Hold... And then release...

Breathe in... Hold... And then release...

Now start to notice the rest of the things that the light and fire touches... Notice your periphery start to become just a little bit visible... It is the light of the candle that is making this happen... Notice also the melted wax of the candle... See it melt... See it drip on the sides of the candle... And notice how the wick holds the fire... The wick is steady... It does not disintegrate even with the great heat of the fire... Notice these things... These are the effects of the candle...

And now it's time to dig deeper and start to feel the sensations and emotions that the candle brings... What can you feel in the darkness? And what can you feel with the light of the candle? Feel the sensations that the candle brings in consonance with the darkness... Feel also the emotions... Let them swirl and capture you... Let these emotions become one with you...

Focus on the light of the candle... Focus on the heat that the fire gives... Feel it and feel yourself live... This is your life... The light and the fire represent your life... This is the message of the candle... Let it remind you of how it is to live... Let it remind you to be in the here and now...

Be in the here and now... In the here and now you burn bright... In the here and now you give off warmth... In the here and now you give off energy... The energy you give off is your spirit... Let your spirit burn bright... So that others can see it more clearly... Let your spirit radiate warmth... So that others can feel and appreciate your presence more... Live life like a candle... Live life like a candle that burns in the here and now...

Breathe in... Hold... And then release...

Breathe in... Hold... And then release...

Breathe in... Hold... And then release...

You are now feeling calm... The stillness and warmth is making you feel very relaxed... Stay with this feeling and maintain your gaze on the candle... See the candle for what it is... Appreciate it... Take in its beauty, its form, its function... And let the message of the candle echo in your mind...

As you are ready to return, close your eyes... Appreciate the darkness as you keep your eyes closed... You are about to end your candle meditation... When you're ready to end the exercise, blow out your candle... Continue to feel the sensations... Continue to feel relaxed and calm... You may take a few moments to lie down and let your mind and body re-acclimatize to your environment...

DAY 21—GUIDED MEDITATION FOR DEEP SLEEP [30 MINUTES]

Sleep has become such a luxury these days because that even the rich and famous are getting so few of it. And a lot of people are foregoing sleep in favor of work or play. It seems sleep now is getting to be the new hot commodity. But you can actually get a good night's sleep if you wish to. It shouldn't be that hard. You can achieve the required number of hours of slumber per day. All you need to do is to put your mind to it. Your mind is very powerful, and it also needs to rest. This is what sleep gives to your mind. And know that your mind is powerful enough to will itself to sleep. Take the time to practice this deep sleep meditation exercise. You will be doing the body scanning technique to bring you to la-la land in no time.

Start by readying your bedroom for sleep. Make sure your bed is ready. Also make sure that the room is conducive for sleeping. Try to achieve peace and quiet for the night. Turn off or turn down the lights. Change to your pajamas or your sleepwear. Get into a very comfortable position. Get under the covers and get ready to start your meditation.

As you got your surroundings ready, now it's time to get yourself prepared... You have to get ready for sleep. Lie down and achieve a very comfortable position... Adjust your position if you need to... Toss and turn until you achieve the perfect position for sleep... Close your eyes... Start to relax... Let your body slump to the mattress... Start feeling the gentle caress of your sheets... Feel your body adjust to the temperature of the room...

As you achieve this, it's time to take control of your breathing... Bring your awareness to your breathing...

Breathe in... Hold... And then release...

Breathe in... Hold... And then release...

Breathe in... Hold... And then release...

Be methodical in your breathing... Bring in your intentionality with each breath... Take it slow... Let the calmness of your slow breaths reach you... Bring in relaxation and calm with each breath... Start to feel the warm fuzzy sensations... Relax and be calm...

Breathe in... Hold... And then release...

Bring yourself to the most important place and time... This place and time is where you need to be as you get yourself ready for sleep... Be in the here and now... Know deep down inside of you that there is nothing you need to do right now... You just need to breathe calmly. Drift and go with the flow... Let the feeling of sleepiness start to take control... every breath brings sleep closer and closer...

Breathe in... Hold... And then release...

Be in the here and now... Welcome the sleepiness... Allow sleep to touch you... Let it do its magic on your mind and body...

At this point, try to deliberately release your breaths ever more slowly... Take a long and deep breath...

Breathe in... Slowly...

Hold...

And then release... very slowly... Punctuate the release with intent and desire...

Try to prolong the release... Feel even more relaxed as you do so...

And then continue with the pattern... Maintain the rhythm of your breathing... Still breathe with the desire and intentness... Continue to be in the here and now...

Breathe in... Hold... And then release...

You are calm... You are relaxed... Everything around you is quiet... You are shrouded by the darkness that is safe and comforting... You can start to feel the warm touch of sleep...

Continue to feel the relaxation and slowly scan your body... Start from your head and slowly move downward... See your body with your mind's eye... Visualize your forehead, your eyes, your nose, your mouth, your chin... See these parts of your face and head in your mind... Until you reach your neck and shoulders... Observe each part... And then feel the sensations... Take your sweet time... You are in no hurry...

Move your scanning downward... And continue to feel the sensations... Take note of the sensations that you are experiencing while you scan your body...

Arrive at the center of your body... Settle your scan at the level of your stomach and chest, your solar plexus... This is your core... Scan its entirety... Notice your chest and diaphragm's movement... See how they gently rise and fall with your breathing... And continue to feel the sensations.... Remember to not be in a hurry... Take your time as you observe your body...

Breathe in... Hold... And then release...

Now reach the level of your hips... You are now scanning your lower torso... Notice your hips and groin area... See your upper legs... See if you can make out the tiny imperceptible movements that they make... Or just observe their stillness... What sensations do you feel?

Move lower and start to scan your legs... Scan the upper part of it... And then move to your knees... Slowly go down and observe your shin... And then your calf... Go further and you can now scan your feet... Scan even the soles of your feet... These are the legs and feet that held you up the entire day... What sensations do you feel? Be deliberate in your scanning... You want to observe every aspect of your legs... And you want to feel all the sensations... Do this slowly... You can take your time scanning...

Breathe in... Hold... And then release...

And then you can move to your arms... Scan your upper arm... See the muscles of your arm and notice how they are working as you are in the clutches of sleep... Move your way to your hands... Marvel at their beauty... These are the hands that enabled you to do wonderful and meaningful work... What sensations do you feel? Scan your arms and hands slowly... Be deliberate in your scanning... Go ahead, you can take your time...

Go back to the sensations that you felt as you scanned your body... Which parts did you feel tension and tightness? And which parts were most relaxed? Go back to the areas where you felt relaxed... Imagine the feeling of relaxation moving to the other parts... Imagine this relaxation start to invade the tight and tense areas... Let this wonderful feeling pervade... Let relaxation permeate... Let it cover your entire body... Start on the areas with the sensations of calmness and relaxation and let them work their way to the rest of the parts...

Breathe in... Hold... And then release...

Be in the here and now... In the here and now you are calm and relaxed... In the here and now you are very close to sleep... Edging closer by the second... So near you can already feel it....

Breathe in... Hold... And then release...

Now your body is in its most relaxed state... This is what it means to get yourself ready for sleep... Your body is allowing itself to welcome sleep... It is making your body hospitable for sleep... So that sleep can stay longer... So that sleep can work its magic on you... So that you can achieve the deepest and most relaxing sleep...

Your head is feeling ever so light... You can start to feel a delightful sensation on your head... This is sleep making your feel very comfortable... It is starting to work its magic on you... Your whole body is feeling very relaxed... There's no tightness... There's no tension... Your body scan released all the tightness and tension... You just feel light right now... You feel like you are floating on air... You are drifting off to slumber... You are gently being carried by sleep to the land of dreams...

Breathe in... Hold... And then release...

Be in the here and now... The here and now you are in looks very much like a restful state of slumber... The here and now is also a very comforting and relaxing place... It is moving you ever so close to true tranquility... You are very close to achieving the sleep that you desire... You are on your way there... Just a little more and you can have a firm grasp of it...

Breathe in... Hold... And then release...

You are safe and sound where you are... As you drift off to sleep you are filled with such a sense of delight and security... Nothing matters anymore... Everything turns to blank...

Now you can sense the nothingness... Your sense of hearing is slowly drifting away as well... Everything is dark... You feel nothing but warmth, calmness, and relaxation... The world you know is starting to melt away... Welcome to nothingness... Welcome to sleep... Sleep well... Reach into the farthest depths of sleep... Goodnight... Sleep tight...

DAY 22—SELF-HEALING MEDITATION [30 MINUTES]

You will once again tap the power of your mind to allow your body to heal. This is one of the mind's superpowers. And you can use this time and time again to bring you to the brink of health. This self-healing meditation is especially useful if ailments and disease are troubling you. It may not totally take away the pain or heal your right away, but the act of meditating will prime both your mind and body for healing. One benefit of this exercise is that you will instantly feel a little bit better. And sometimes it's just a matter of setting the mood so that you can start to activate your body's self-healing process.

As always, start by settling into your sweet spot. This is the third week of your meditation practice. You should have established your sweet spot by now. Go to this place and start getting comfortable. Place your body in a relaxed position... Let it achieve stillness and calm... You will need this in order for your body to heal...

Once you achieve the relaxed pose, start by bringing your awareness to your breathing... Let all your energy flow through your breathing... Concentrate on it and execute each breath like you mean it... Let air flow in and out of you with great desire... Focus your mind on your body's process of respiration...

Breathe in... Hold... And then release...

Breathe in... Hold... And then release...

Breathe in... Hold... And then release...

Imagine that each breath you take is a cleansing breath... It brings in positive energy... And this positive energy enlivens every cell in your body... It makes your muscles feel more relaxed... And the air you breathed in actually sweeps away the tension and tightness... And as you exhale, it takes with it all the impurities of your body... Your body is cleansed and purified with each breath you take...

Breathe in... Hold... And then release...

Be in the here and now... Let your breathing be the only thing that matters... Let your breathing bring you to the here and now... Allow it to block off all the distractions... Allow it to be the only focus you have... Because breathing is bringing you the good energy... Breathing is what allows your body to be cleansed and purified... This is the reality of the here and now...

Now begin to observe your body... Try to feel the sensations... What is your body trying to tell you? Are there specific parts that call out to you? Where are these parts? Can you try to identify them?

Breathe in... Hold... And then release...

What are they trying to tell you? Are you sensing some discomfort in these parts? Or worse, are you feeling pain? Is there something wrong with that body part? Is it not functioning well enough? What is stopping these parts from being at their best? Try to feel these sensations... Feel what these body parts are feeling... Don't be afraid of them... They are part of you anyway...

Feel the discomfort... Feel the pain... Know that they are part of you... There's a reason why they're there... There's a reason why you're feeling them right now... This is part of the here and now... Go ahead and feel them... Experience every sensation....

Now go back to your breathing...

Breathe in... Hold... And then release...

Breathe in... Hold... And then release...

Breathe in... Hold... And then release...

Bring your awareness back to the air that surrounds you... This is the cleansing and purifying air... This is the air that is needed for your body to start its healing process... Appreciate the fact that this cleansing and purifying air is all around you... It is yours for the taking... All you have to do is to want it... So be deliberate in your breathing... Desire every breath... Make sure you get all the air you need... So that your body can start healing... So that your mind can also start healing...

Breathe in... Hold... And then release...

Breathe in... Slowly...

Hold... Make sure to let the air circulate inside you...

And then release... Very slowly once again... Let your exhalation bring out the discomfort and pain that you are feeling...

Now feel the cleansing and purifying air start to work their way on your feet... They start at your soles and you can feel them on your toes... There's a warm feeling to them... It tingles... And it tickles a bit... You enjoy the feeling... It is in stark contrast to the pain and discomfort you felt in the other areas...

This warm, wonderful feeling starts to spread... It starts to move its way up... You can now feel it on your legs... And it somehow starts to take away some of the discomfort and pain... This energy is slowly substituting all the bad sensations... It is replacing it with a certain kind of warmth...

The pain and discomfort are still there... It did not go away entirely... But the energy is trying to make it more tolerable... You can stand the pain and discomfort now... Its intensity has greatly diminished... It makes you feel all the more relaxed... You appreciate being momentarily released from the clutches of pain and discomfort...

It feels liberating... And you want it to continue... And this energy, the air that you breathe is moving once again... It reaches your lower torso and it does its magic there also... The pain and discomfort are waning... You start to feel whole again... You are now reminiscing the time when you were at your peak health-wise....

Breathe in... Hold... And then release...

Breathe in... Hold... And then release...

Breathe in... Hold... And then release...

Start to feel this energy rising above your ankles, flowing up your lower legs... And then it reaches your knees.... Until it makes its way up to your upper legs... Allow the relaxation that the energy brings to continue to spread throughout your body... It is now trying to reach your hips... Soon you can feel it reach your pelvis... And then it settles on your stomach...

You continue to take in all the positivity from this... You are enjoying the feeling of having the discomfort and pain subside... You look forward to having more of it... You know that the air you take in is promising you more relief... You know you can look forward to more healing and recovery... Your body is actually starting to heal...

From your stomach, it is now making its way to your chest... And then you can start to feel it on your back... It is hitting your core... It is bringing you back the balance you once lost... You can feel whole again... All these feelings of healing and recovery are being brought about by the air you breathe... Continue to bring in desire with every breath...

Breathe in... Hold... And then release...

It flows now to your arms... It has made its way up to your elbows... You can start to feel the energy bring its vibe to your wrist... Soon your hands and filled with this energy... It spreads even to your fingers... It is starting to cover your entire body... And the delightful sensations just put you in a more relaxed state... Let the calmness take over...

Now this healing energy that comes from the air you breathe is making its way to its final destination... It slowly climbs up to your head... You can now feel the muscles of your face start to soften... You are now smiling... This is the effect of healing on you... Your neck and shoulders are also very relaxed now...

You can feel it in your eyes now... Even if your eyes are closed, you can feel it... It touches your eyelids as it makes its way ever upward... And now it settles on your forehead... You can feel the energy hover above your head now... You can sense its warmth as it tries to decompress all the unnecessary thoughts... It is also healing your mind now... You can feel a certain lightness overtake you... This is the lightness that is borne out of healing... And you heal yourself as you breathe... You are bringing the healing energy inside your body with each breath you take...

Breathe in... Hold... And then release...

Breathe in... Hold... And then release...

Breathe in... Hold... And then release...

Be in the here and now... The here and now is the time and place where healing can take place... Stay in this moment... And know that you can go to this place and time anytime you wish... Know that your body is capable of healing itself... All you need is the time and place... All you need to do is to be in the here and now...

Maintain the relaxing feeling you have established as your body is trying to heal itself... Feel jubilant at your body's great ability to heal, recharge, and recuperate... Continue to feel the calm... Continue to feel at ease... Maintain that confidence you feel right now as you are allowing your body to heal...

You are now ready to return... Feel free to shake off the relaxation a bit by doing some slight movements... This will bring life back to your relaxed muscles... You can even do some stretching poses... And if you are ready, you can open your eyes...

Or feel free to maximize your current blissful feeling... You can continue to feel relaxed and calm... You can also continue to let your body heal a little bit more... Know that this process takes time... It is best to let your healing continue... It should not be rushed... This process should be unhurried...

DAY 23—STRESS RELIEF MEDITATION: LOOKING AT THE STARS [30 MINUTES]

Another wonder that's always available to us is the stars. They should be visible and bright on a clear night. The stars give you a sense of awe. There is a mystery to them that awakens the curious mind. This mystery and wonder have transfixed a lot of people to the night sky, hoping to catch a glimpse of the constellation of stars. By looking up in the night sky, you can attain a form of peace. You can gaze to the stars and appreciate them in their majestic beauty and splendor. Try this meditation exercise tonight.

You need to be outdoors for this exercise. It is with great hope that the weather will cooperate. Go out under the night sky and find for yourself a place where you can be seated comfortably. Or, if you prefer, you can lie down for this exercise. Find a place that is dark so that you can get a better view of the stars. Settle down and get yourself in your most comfortable position.

Let your eyes adjust to the darkness as you become more comfortable in your position. Feel the night breeze try to cool you down… And try to distance yourself from the noise that you may hear on your periphery… Detach yourself from the world… Now it's just you and the night sky… And the sky is offering you thousands, if not millions, of stars… They are all right there above you… Behold the stars of the night sky…

As you take in the view of the stars, try to gain awareness of your breathing... Be aware of how the air flows in and out of your body... Try to visualize their path as they enter and leave your body... Be deliberate in your breathing... Try to put your whole self into your breathing...

Breathe in... Hold... And then release...

Breathe in... Hold... And then release...

Breathe in... Hold... And then release...

Maintain your focus on the sky and the stars as you breathe... Let the air around you energize you... Visualize its flow... See with your mind's eye how the air is entering your body... See how it circulates inside of you... And then see it leave you... Watch the air as it returns to its starting point...

Breathe in... Take a look at the sky... Appreciate its vastness... Try to fathom what you can see before you... Try to fathom how vast it is... Try and see if you can comprehend its limitlessness...

Hold your breath for a few moments... See the stars... There are a myriad stars out before you...

And then release... A million tiny specs of light out there in the vastness of space... See them twinkle, see them shine, see them sparkle... The night sky comes alive with the stars out and about... They are like a hundred thousand diamonds on the night sky... Their tiny but powerful light punctuates the darkness of space...

Be deliberate in the way you breathe... Bring in all of your energy into your breathing... Let your whole being breathe with you... And as you do, appreciate the beauty of the darkened sky that is above you... Desire every breath you take... And use this same desire in your observation and appreciation of the stars...

Breathe in... Hold... And then release...

See the stars up above... Watch how they brighten the sky up above you... It's not totally black... You can see the light of the moon... And you can see the light of the stars...

These stars are twinkling... All stars flicker... Their interplay of light and dark makes it seem like they are blinking... And you can faintly see different colors as the stars sparkle... Try to make out the yellows and the oranges... And the reds and the purples... And even the blues... Try to spot a star giving out a blue twinkle...

See the majesty of the constellation... This is the same constellation your forefathers viewed... This is the same night sky your ancestors saw when they looked up... Appreciate this fact... Appreciate the fact that you have something you can share with your forefathers and ancestors... The night sky has always been there... It's been there through time... And will always be there in the days to come...

Let the night sky remind you of the here and now... Let the darkness of night bring you to the only place and time that matters... Let the light of the stars that dance on the dark canvass of the sky remind you that the only place and time you need to at is the here and now...

Be in the here and now... This is what the night sky is telling you... This is the message the stars are trying to impress on you... Remember that they have been there since the dawn of time... And as always, the night sky and the stars remain there... To your eyes, they will always be in the here and now... Even though they are quite far... so far away... and they are from another time... a distance so far...

But be in the here and now... And look at the stars as they twinkle... Relive the time when you were a child... Remember the old nursery rhyme...

Look up the night sky and start to wonder... Wonder what they are... Think about the stars and what they mean to you... Think about them because they are trying to tell a story... They are sending a message to you...

Be in the here and now as you gaze at the stars... And let the stars do their nightly light performance...

Breathe in... Hold... And then release...

Breathe in... Hold... And then release...

Breathe in... Hold... And then release...

Now feel the sensation that is entering your body... What feelings are starting to feel? Can you feel the calm and stillness that the night sky and stars are giving? Try to let the view relax you... It is a view of peace... It should make you feel at ease... You are watching a spectacle of light... Appreciate the interplay of light and dark as you gaze at the night sky...

Experience wave after wave of rejuvenating energy flow through you... This is the effect of the calm and stillness that you are feeling... This is what the stars of the night offer you... Let it whisper in your ear that nothing matters... Nothing matters in the here and now... All you have to do is to look up... All you have to do is to keep your eyes open... And see the stars... See them shine brightly... Like a thousand tiny diamonds in the sky...

Breathe in... Hold... And then release...

Breathe in... Hold... And then release...

Breathe in... Hold... And then release...

Continue to be amazed at what you are seeing... Feel the joy that this spectacle brings... Count yourself lucky that you can open your eyes and see the stars... Feel blessed at being able to go out at night and be right under the stars...

Bask in the light of the night sky... Let the light that illuminates the darkness of night bathe you... Feel its presence... Feel its power... Let it transport you to the here and now... This is the power of the light of the night sky... Let the sparkling dazzling light bring you to the only place and time that matters...

Be in the here and now...

Revel in the stillness and the calm...

Appreciate the light show in front of you...

The stars are out tonight... And they dance... They burn brightly... They do this for you... So that you are reminded of your existence... So that you can once again bring yourself to the here and now...

Try to look at the stars more intently this time... Etch them to memory... Try to see their image even as you close your eyes... Let their light continue to shine even with your eyes closed...

And then just take a moment... Pause... Take a moment to be with the night sky... Take a moment to be with the stars... Take a moment to be in the here and now... Pause... And take your time... You are in no hurry... The stars are in no hurry as well... They have existed for eons... And they will continue to exist for eons more... They are not going anywhere... So just take it in... Take all of it in...

Breathe in... Hold... And then release...

Breathe in... Hold... And then release...

Breathe in... Hold... And then release...

Once you are ready to return, open your eyes... Move your arms and legs... You can even do some light stretches... Bring your senses back by putting some form of motion to your body...

You can once again see the beauty of the night sky and the stars... Feel free to stay where you are... You can continue to gaze at the stars... Again, there is no need to hurry... You can take your time... Tonight, it's just you and the stars...

DAY 24—BEFORE SLEEP DEEP RELAXATION MEDITATION: REFLECTING ON YOUR JOURNEY [30 MINUTES]

It's always advisable to take the time to reflect on your life. You can gain a lot of insight as you continue your journey. And it is also refreshing and relaxing to do as well. This exercise can be done just as you are about to sleep. The lightness of the mood you will be experiencing while doing this exercise will help bring you pleasant sleep. Prepare yourself for a night of relaxing and restful slumber.

First, prepare your bedroom. It's always best to make sure that your rest area is conducive to sleep. Set the temperature of the room just right—not too cold, not to warm. Turn off the lights or you can just dim them if you are uncomfortable with total darkness. Wear your sleep clothes—clothing that is loose and that will allow your body to be comfortable.

Settle into your bed and try to attain a very comfortable position... Go ahead and toss and turn a little bit... Try to find that sweet spot... Try to achieve the perfect position... Once you feel relaxed and calm, you may begin with the exercise... Close your eyes...

Feel the stillness of the bedroom... Realize that it is late at night... The world is also calling it a day... It's time for rest... It's time for you to go to sleep...

You find yourself in a very comfortable space... You are in your bedroom... You are lying down in your bed... You know these spaces very well... These are safe spaces... These spaces allow you to rest... So go ahead and let your weary mind and body rest...

Try to focus on your breathing... Let your breathing bring you relaxation... Let it bring you calmness... Let your breathing create stillness in your mind and body...

Breathe in... Hold... And then release...

Each breath is a breath of relaxation... You are taking in relaxation... Take more of it...

Breathe in... Hold... And then release...

You feel more and more relaxed... You can sense a certain warmth that tries to envelop your whole body... The air you breathe is letting this warm feeling spread all throughout your body... Your muscles now feel loose... There is nary a sign of tension in them... The tightness you earlier felt is all but gone... Your whole body now feels light... It feels like you are floating on air... And that your body is perched on a soft fluffy cloud which is your bed...

Let these feelings run through you... Enjoy the sensations... These are the sensations of relaxation... These feelings are brought about as you take in more of the relaxing air you breathe...

Breathe in... Hold... And then release...

Breathe in... Hold... And then release...

Breathe in... Hold... And then release...

As you continue to enjoy the wonderful sensations, try to bring yourself to the here and now... Let your breathing help you with this... The here and now is where you want to be... It is the only place and time that matters...

Realize that you are calm and still in the here and now... Realize that you have decided to set aside all cares and worries... You do not need those in the here and now... You can set them aside for now because they have no place as you sleep... As you try to attain peaceful slumber, you only need to be present... Just be in the here and now...

Breathe in... Hold... And then release...

Breathe in... Hold... And then release...

Breathe in... Hold... And then release...

Nothing else matters in the here and now... It is just you and your breathing... It is just you feeling very relaxed... very still... very calm...

And now it's time to think about your life... Reflect on your journey... Try to bring back all of your achievements as you traversed through the road of life ... Take the time to relive and remember these memories...

Know that you have accomplished a lot... And know that you have a lot more to accomplish... Think about these accomplishments for a moment... Try to bring yourself back when these happened... Relish at the joy you felt when you experienced these accomplishments... See in your mind's eye how happy you were then...

And then think of the people that helped you get to where you are right now... These are the people that are important to you... These are the people that matter... Fill your heart with gratitude as you try to conjure their images in your mind... Be thankful that you crossed paths with these individuals... As they made an impact on you, you also made an impact on them....

Get a good sense of how wonderful your life has been, even with all the ups and downs... The fact that you are breathing is already a testament to life's greatness... The fact that you can be in the here and now means that your existence matters... Try to capture the entirety of the greatness of your existence in your thoughts...

Dwell on the positives... And know that you will have more opportunities in store for you tomorrow... For tomorrow is another day...

Realize that your struggles and challenges have a purpose... This is part of your journey... They give more meaning to your life... Take these in as well... Let these struggles and challenges enrich you... Take them wholeheartedly and also appreciate them...

Breathe in... Hold... And then release...

Fill your heart with gladness and content as you reflect on your journey... Your journey thus far has put you in the most important spot—the here and now... The here and now offers boundless opportunities... There are countless more chapters to write in the book of life...

But those are for another day... Right now, what is important is that you are filled with a spirit of gratitude... You took the time to reflect and it has brought you to a place and time that is filled with longing and love... Enjoy this moment... Put these thoughts in the backseat... You can always look at the rear-view mirror to see these thoughts... This is how you reflect on your life...

Return to the here and now... But know that you can always glance at the rear-view mirror... Do this if you want to reflect on the life you lived thus far... But right now, be in the here and now... Achieve this with your breathing...

Breathe in... Hold... And then release...

Breathe in... Hold... And then release...

Breathe in... Hold... And then release...

In the here and now everything is still... The night is still... The world is still... Your body is still... and so is your mind... Your heart is filled with joy and gratitude... In the here and now, you are ready for sleep...

So welcome sleep... You can let go of wakefulness now... It's time for you to rest... Welcome sleep and let it be part of your here and now...

Breathe in... Hold... And then release...

Breathe in... Hold... And then release...

Each breath is making you feel more relaxed... Each breath brings you closer to sleep...

Breathe in... Hold... And then release...

Breathe in... Hold... And then release...

Allow yourself to drift to sleep... Loosen your grip with the conscious waking world... You can let go of it now... You were awake for much of the day... You devoted the majority of your time to achieve your goals... It's time to rest... It's time to let your body recuperate... It's time to let your mind decompress...

But maintain the feeling of calmness and joy... Let the positivity continue to surround you... These feelings will bring you a kind of sleep that is more restful... It will allow you to go deeper and deeper into your sleep... This is the sleep that you want... This is the sleep that you deserve... So claim it... Prime yourself for deep sleep... Prepare yourself for a night of truly restful slumber...

Breathe in... Hold... And then release...

Breathe in... Hold... And then release...

Breathe in... Hold... And then release...

What matters now is just you drifting off to unconsciousness with a thankful heart... This is the here and now that you find yourself in...

Release your grip of consciousness... Give in to sleep...

This meditation exercise is about to end... It will end at the count of 3...

3...

2...

1...

Good night...

DAY 25—RELAXED MINDFUL EATING: GUIDED MINDFULNESS TO APPRECIATE YOUR MEAL BETTER [30 MINUTES]

This is a special exercise that will break your usual dining routine. Mindful eating is getting to be more popular nowadays. This experience will bring you closer to the food that you are eating. You can prepare a special meal or just a simple one. Know that the type of food or dish does not matter much in this exercise. This is all about the journey. Getting to your desired destination will just be the icing on the cake—a cherry to top this proverbial sundae. This is all about learning to appreciate the food you are eating—the meal you are partaking in—through mindfulness. You can experience a higher level of delight and satisfaction with your food if you are more mindful of it.

To start with, make sure that you have everything prepared. The easiest would be to order food from a restaurant. But you can also cook and prepare your own food for this exercise. Cooking your own food will bring a deeper mindfulness dimension into this whole experience. Settle down on the table and get yourself in a comfortable position. Get ready to start your mindful eating journey.

You can start by connecting your breath and body...

Breathe in... Hold... And then release...

Get a full sense of how your body is feeling right at this very moment... Become aware of the sensations that are coursing through you... Become aware as well of the many behaviors your body is doing at this point... Notice the tiny gestures, the twitches, or even the grumbling of your stomach... These are the usual reactions to hunger... You must surely be manifesting these reactions by now...

Next, try to dig deep and notice the emotions that you are feeling at this very moment... How do you feel inside? Do you feel the anticipation? Do feel the excitement? What thoughts and feelings do you have right now knowing that you are about to partake in a meal? Take the time to feel and to let these emotions emerge...

Breathe in... Hold... And then release...

Keep your body and breath connected... Stay conscious of this... This will allow you to stay in the here and now... You need to be in the here and now to be mindful of your meal... This will let you appreciate your meal more...

Be in the here and now...

You must be feeling very hungry now... The anticipation is building... Tune in to this awareness of hunger... Can you feel the pangs? How about thirst? Do you feel the need to drink? What thoughts dominate your mind right now? Try to understand the act of eating and drinking... And further this understanding by asking yourself why you are eating what you eat... And why you are drinking what you drink... Take time to ask these things.... And take time to answer...

Know the purpose of your meal... Is it merely sustenance? Or is there something more to this meal than just for food and drink to fill you? Is this meal a journey into pleasure? Is this meal about making you feel good inside and out? Or is there a social aspect to the meal? Are you enjoying the meal with people? Who are these people? And why do they matter?

Go ahead and think of these things... Let these thoughts marinate... Let them enhance your experience as you partake in your meal...

Breathe in... Hold... And then release...

It's time to eat... But before doing so, try to handle the food that's in front of you... Go ahead and touch it... Take it... Put it on your palm... Hold the food... Try to let your curiosity run wild as you hold this piece of gastronomical delight... Observe with all your senses everything about it... From its shape, size, color, texture... Observe it...

And then become aware of the sensations and feelings that come about from your observation... How does this make you feel? How does it feel to put the food you eat on your hands? Take some time to think about this...

Breathe in... Hold... And then release...

It's time to taste the food... Go ahead and put it in your mouth... Be very deliberate when you do this... As you put it in your mouth, let its aroma tickle your nose... Let its fine odor enhance your experience... Its aroma is supposed to heighten your other senses...

Breathe in... Hold... And then release...

Try to let the food touch your lips first... Let its warm temperature kiss your lips as you start to put it inside your mouth... And once it is inside your mouth, take the time to really taste it... Taste it for all its worth... Let the flavors burst in your mouth... Let your tongue marvel at the wonderful sensations it is feeling...

What flavors can you sense? What different textures are present in your mouth right now? Go ahead and name them all... Feel a certain form of satisfaction emerge as you experience all the different flavors and textures in your mouth...

Start chewing the food... Feel more bursts of flavor as your teeth and mouth do their work of breaking the food down... Chew slowly... Make sure that you can really experience all the wonderful flavors of the food... Appreciate as well the changes in texture as you chew...

And then when the food has been broken down to a much smaller piece, swallow it... Let it dance around your throat as you swallow... And when it finally settles down in your stomach, feel the delight... You have just eaten mindfully... You took the time and effort to really appreciate the food that you are eating...

Breathe in... Hold... And then release... Remember to be in the here and now... In the here and now you are being nourished by nutritious and delicious food... And you appreciate every morsel... You took the time to bring out all the goodness in it... Each bite, each chew, each swallow has become such a delightful experience...

Breathe in... Hold... And then release...

And as the food settles in your stomach, take time to appreciate its journey... Realize that the food you see in front of you now underwent several transformations... It went through a process of preparation... And now it has been transformed into a delightful dish that you can enjoy to your heart's content... Appreciate your food's journey from farm to table...

Also appreciate the hands that shaped and formed the food you have before you... These hands belong to hardworking people... These are the farmers, delivery persons, cooks... These people were instrumental in bringing that delicious dish that is in front of you right now... Appreciate these loving hands...

Breathe in... Hold... And then release...

Take another bite... Go ahead and eat once again... What memories were conjured as you ate the food? Did it bring you back to your childhood? Were memories of the past brought back as you bit into your food? Or did it bring other more recent memories? Know that food has this power... Food can connect the past to the present... Take the time to relive these memories through the food you eat... Let past happiness re-emerge each time you partake of the food...

Breathe in... Hold... And then release...

Go ahead and build a steady rhythm of eating... Eat slow... Take the time to really appreciate each morsel of food you put in your mouth... This is how to eat mindfully... And it is a wonderful way to eat... Does your food taste much better if you are more mindful of it? Enjoy the sensations... Reminisce about the happy memories it brought... And let it nourish you... Let it remind you that life is great... Let it remind you that you are here to live... You are here to live in the here and now...

And in the here and now you are being nourished by wonderful and delicious food... Food that was methodically and meticulously prepared by hardworking and loving hands... Food that brings back memories—happy memories... This is the here and now...

Breathe in... Hold... And then release...

Breathe in... Hold... And then release...

Breathe in... Hold... And then release...

Remain in the here and now for the course of your meal...

You are now at the conclusion of your mindfulness eating exercise... But go ahead and continue with your meal... Eat heartily... Eat with joy... And eat slowly... Maintain mindfulness with each bite... Food tastes so much better this way... Bon appetit!

DAY 26—MORNING ANXIETY-REDUCING MEDITATION TO KICK-START YOUR DAY [30 MINUTES]

Mornings are a difficult period energy-wise, especially if you woke up on the wrong side of the bed. Don't worry, you can just kick-start your own internal engine—your mind. Your mind is a powerful organ that can enable itself to create energy. All you need to do is to tap this energy reservoir that is already inside of you. And you can achieve this through meditation and mindfulness. This exercise aims to do just that. So get ready to jumpstart your day and get the right amount of energy you need.

The most important thing about this exercise is that you do this very early in the morning... Start when the sun has not yet risen... You will certainly still feel tired and sluggish, but this is part of the experience... You will learn to appreciate more your renewed energy at the end of the exercise if you start early in the day... So get up while the sun has not yet risen...

Pull yourself up from your bed... Do this with great desire even if your bed still calls for you... Resist the temptation to go back to bed... Doing so will kill the intent of this whole exercise... Put some life into your limbs and bones... Rise even if your muscles are not cooperating... Get up... Stand up... Start your day while the sun has not yet started its day....

Try to shake some of the sluggishness off if you can... It's perfectly normal for you to feel like this... After all, you just woke up... And it's so early... But put some energy into your body... It may feel difficult since your energy is in such short supply... But do it anyway...

Straighten your back as you stand... Achieve a good posture... This will surely bring you more energy... And then stretch your arms and legs... Feel the muscles stretch and then relax... Stretch until you can start to feel the muscles warm up...

Bring in desire into each of your movements... You can take your time introducing energy into your body... Do it slowly so that you can ease your way into things... There is no need to do things quickly... The day is still early... You have time for this... You have time to be slow and methodical in bringing your energy levels up...

Start to bring your focus and attention to your breathing... Channel the same desire and intentness you showed earlier to your breath... And feel the added energy that each breath brings...

Breathe in... Hold... And then release...

The tiredness is starting to leave you a little bit... Your head does not feel as heavy as it did when you woke up...

Breathe in... Hold... And then release...

In your wakefulness, you have achieved being in the only place and time that matters... You are in the here and now... And each energetic breath you take brings you to the here and now...

Continue to concentrate on your breathing... Know that your breathing is your key to getting your energy levels up... Your breathing is the key to the ignition... You can fire up your internal engine once you turn the key... Let your breathing enable you to power this engine... So concentrate... Bring in that desire, that intentness...

Breathe in... Hold... And then release...

Breathe in... Hold... And then release...

Breathe in... Hold... And then release...

Prepare yourself, now it's time to turn on the engine... Picture yourself holding the key to the engine... Again, the key is your breathing... You have a firm grasp on it... You are doing it in full concentration... You can feel the desire and intentness with each breath...

Imagine yourself putting the key in the slot... It fits perfectly...

Breathe in... Hold... And then release...

Turn the key... Visualize yourself carefully turning the key... You hear a sound... It's the sound of an engine trying to will itself to life... You put more pressure on the key as you turn it... Picture yourself putting this pressure on the key...

Breathe in... Hold... And then release...

Until you hear a roar! The roar is from your internal engine... You have successfully started it... It roars to life... Its roar is loud... Its roar is proud... It makes an announcement to the whole world... It shouts and screams energy... It starts to pulsate life and vigor... This is your internal engine... And you have kick-started it...

Breathe in... Hold... And then release...

Breathe in... Hold... And then release...

Breathe in... Hold... And then release...

Each breath you take feeds fuel to your internal engine... It is revving more and more... You can feel the power surge... You can feel the energy surge within you... Let this energy continue to grow... Let your engine continue to rev...

You can now feel a sudden rise in temperature... This is the energy that your internal engine produces... Your muscles do not feel listless anymore... On the contrary, they are now full of life... They are ready to move... They are ready for a day full of work... They are ready to let you achieve your goals for the day...

And your head is getting a buzz of great awareness... The energy you are manufacturing from within you is allowing your mind to focus... And it is now focusing on what is important... It is focusing on providing you with more energy... It is focusing on being in the here and now...

Breathe in... Hold... And then release...

Imagine yourself pulsating to the hum of your internal engine... You are revving and vibrating... You are now full of kinetic energy... You are full of anticipation now... You can't wait to get started... You can't wait to move... You have the energy... You have now a good supply of it...

Breathe in... Hold... And then release...

Breathe in... Hold... And then release...

Breathe in... Hold... And then release...

Bring back your focus on your breathing... Your breathing was the key in kick-starting your engine... And it remains the key now for you to feed more fuel to let your engine burn more energy... So continue your focus... Keep your awareness centered on your breathing...

Each breath brings more energy to your being... Let more energy flow into you... Achieve this with each breath that you take in... Do it with great desire...

Your breath and the energy it brings allows you to remain in the here and now... In the here and now you are brimming with energy... In the here and now you are ready to take on the day... In the here and now, you have the capacity to increase your energy levels...

At this point, you should be free from your anxieties... By triggering the ignition of your internal engine, you allowed yourself to get the energy you need... This allowed you to be in the here and now... And in the here and now all your cares and worries do not matter... What matters in the here and now is that you are brimming with life...

Put your cares and worries in the background... Know that thoughts of the past are but memories... They cease to matter in the here and now... And know that thoughts of the future are mere projections... They have not formed any semblance of value yet in the here and now... These things do not matter... The only thing that matters is your energy... It is one with your breathing...

Try to imagine your head now... Imagine it free of the anxieties that haunted you earlier... Your head feels a sense of liberation... It feels light... It can now absorb the energy... Your head is clear... Your mind is ready to take on the challenges the day will bring... It is primed to be at its best...

Breathe in... Hold... And then release...

Each breath not only brings you more energy, but it also puts your anxieties in the background... Be one with your breathing... And just allow the energy to flow... Let the energy power you as you remain in the here and now...

Breathe in... Hold... And then release...

Time to get started... Time to get a move on... You are more than ready to start your day... Your energy level has greatly increased... And it continues to rise... You have successfully kick-started your morning... Try to jump around... Try to jog in place... Shake those energetic arms and legs... Bring more energy to your body...

You can now face the world... Go out of your room... Time to leave your safe place... You are now more than capable of meeting the demands of the day...

DAY 27—GUIDED MEDITATION FOR REDUCING ANXIETY: LISTENING TO THE WIND [30 MINUTES]

Feeling the wind can give you a very relaxing feeling. It also soothes and refreshes you. This exercise will let you experience the goodness of a cool breeze. You can certainly feel the refreshing power of the wind. This exercise will enable you to further practice your mindfulness habit.

This exercise requires you to be outdoors as you need to be able to feel the wind blow. Find a suitable location, preferably a place that you can be alone. It helps if this place is quiet. You want to maximize the experience by being in a place that offers you peace and tranquility. And you can do this any time of the day. But the best time to do this will be early in the morning or during night time after dinner.

Start by going outside and settle into position. Get comfortable and start to let the environment relax you. Sit comfortably but make sure that your back is straight. Or better yet, you can lie down if you can find the opportunity for this. Just make sure that your back is straight the whole time and that your body is not arched in an awkward position. And as you attain relaxation, close your eyes.

Start to feel the air around you... And then bring your attention to your breathing... Be one with your breath...

Bring your whole being with you as you breathe... Put in your whole spirit as you execute each inhalation and exhalation... Desire each breath... Want it... Put your whole self in it... Let your spirit flow with your breath...

Breathe in... Hold... And then release...

Let relaxation flow with each breath... Feel the calmness start to overcome your whole body... And let all the tension and tightness escape as you exhale...

Maintain your concentration... Be one with your breath... Be deliberate with each breath... Let each breath be an intentional desire on your part...

Let your breath remind you to be in the here and now... You are in the here and now... And the only thing that matters is you just existing in this time and place... It's just you and your breath... That is your reality... Your reality in the here and now...

Start to feel your surroundings... Can you feel the wind blow? Can you feel the wind's soft touch? Its coolness is slowly caressing your skin... It cools you down, bringing your internal temperature lower... It refreshes you... Feel the relaxation increase as you experience the breeze dancing all around you...

And as you feel the wind, let your breathing flow with it... Let your breathing and the wind flow in unison...

Breathe in... Hold... And then release...

What sensations do you feel as the wind is blowing? What feelings do you derive from the wind touching you? Aside from its cooling effect, what things are brought about by the wind? Let the wind offer you its gifts... Feel them, embrace them... Accept these gifts that the wind brings...

Breathe in... Hold... And then release...

Remember to breathe in unison with the wind's movements... Remember to be in the here and now... This is your reality... You are experiencing the joy of being one with the wind...

Try to rekindle happy memories as the gust of wind blows by you... What do you remember as you feel the refreshing wind pass you by? Try your best to conjure all the delightful memories... These memories are also the wind's gift to you... Take them, accept them... Try to remember... Picture these events in your mind's eye...

Breathe in... Hold... And then release...

Remember to be in the here and now... This is the only place and time that matters...

In the here and now, the wind blows away all the cobwebs that are present in your mind... These cobwebs are your cares and worries... They are your anxieties... Allow the wind to sweep these anxieties away... Let the wind take these apprehensions... There's certainly no need for you to hold on to them... Let these angsts, fears, concerns, and unease disintegrate as they are swept away by the wind... This is another gift that the wind brings you... Accept this gift...

And now you have to listen to what the wind is saying... What is it telling you? What is its message? Go ahead... Try to listen... Train your ears well... Listen carefully... Listen intently... It gives you a soft whisper... It makes the faintest sound, yet this sound reverberates in your mind and heart... Listen to the wind... Listen to what it has to say...

Breathe in... Hold... And then release...

The wind is telling you to let go of the past... The wind is telling you to disregard the future... These things are not in the here and now... They have ceased to matter... Or they do not matter yet... There is no need to let these things invade your thoughts... Listen to the wind... Listen to what it has to say...

And then there is the song that the wind is singing... It is singing a comforting tune... It puts your mind at ease... It sings a song that puts peace in your heart... It sings a song that clears your mind... It is easy on the ears... This song delights your soul... Listen to the song of the wind... And if you can, try to sing along... The tune is familiar to you... You know the words... Go ahead and sing along...

The wind is also giving you advice... Listen to its wisdom... The wind is telling you to go live your life... To just be in the here and now... It assures you that it will be there for you when you need it... The wind will always find a way to sweep your anxieties away... All you need to do is to call for it... All you need to do is to concentrate on your breathing...

Breathe in... Hold... And then release...

Breathe in... Hold... And then release...

Breathe in... Hold... And then release...

You are in the here and now... And in this time and place, you are communing with the wind... You are listening to its whisper... And you are singing a duet with it... It is a song of peace and love... This song takes away all your cares and worries...

Feel the positive effects of your endeavor... The wind has brought you to a very relaxed state... You are in a state of calm... And you feel very refreshed... You are thoroughly enjoying the experience... You are taking full advantage of the wind and its gifts to you...

Go ahead and enjoy the wind... Know that you are in no hurry... So take your time... Commune with the wind... Let your soul continue to communicate with it...

Let your body experience the refreshing feeling of having been recharged by the wind... Feel your energy and power surge as the wind's current around you intensifies... Feel your soul come alive... And let the happy memories flow... Take all of this in and just go with the flow of the wind...

Breathe in... Hold... And then release...

Breathe in... Hold... And then release...

Breathe in... Hold... And then release...

Continue to let your breathing be your focus as you commune with the wind... Take your time... You are in no hurry... Just go with the flow...

You are about to put this meditation exercise to a close... You had a wonderful moment with the wind... Take a few more moments to commune with it... Try to feel its coolness a little bit more... Listen to what it is trying to say one last time... And then thank the wind... Thank the wind for bestowing you its gifts... And make sure to bring these gifts with you as you go...

Breathe in... Hold... And then release...

Breathe in... Hold... And then release...

Breathe in... Hold... And then release...

Maintain the feelings of relaxation and calm... And continue to situate yourself in the here and now...

This exercise has reached its terminus... Get ready to return... As you do, take with you the gifts... And continue to feel relaxed... You will go about your way and return to where you started at the count of three...

Three...

Two...

One...

You may now open your eyes and move your body...

Welcome back!

DAY 28—STRESS-RELIEVING GUIDED MEDITATION—OVERCOMING CHRONIC FATIGUE [30 MINUTES]

Fatigue or extreme tiredness is a normal reaction to stress. As you subject your body to a lot of stress, your body gets tired over time. But to feel this extreme form of tiredness for prolonged periods is not normal anymore. You may be suffering from Chronic Fatigue Syndrome. But know that you can do something about this. You can channel your energy within to properly deal with the stress that you are feeling. In turn, you just might be able to reduce the fatigue and tiredness plaguing you. Try this meditation exercise and reap the benefits of stress relief. You may just discover your fatigue dissipate and your energy levels increased.

Find a comfortable position once again. Go to your identified spot for meditation and make sure this place can give you the peace and quiet you need for this exercise. The best position for your body for this exercise is sitting down. You may sit cross-legged. Just make sure your back is not arched as you do this exercise. Keep your shoulders and neck relaxed. Ease the tensions you feel in these areas of your body. Keep your hands on your lap and let them rest there. Close your eyes and prepare to begin.

You have been feeling very tired lately… In fact, this weariness is starting to affect you… It's bringing you down… It's starting to take a toll on your work… on your life... on your daily existence... You feel this fatigue weighing you down heavily... It is a colossal burden to carry... It adds an additional layer of complication to your already challenging life... And yet the stress continues to pile up... This is because the demands are great... Every single day requires you to be at your best... To put your best foot forward... And you are more than willing to meet and even exceed those demands...

And this causes you a lot of stress... And now you are at the depths of tiredness... You are very fatigued...

Acknowledge this tiredness... Let the weariness out... Feel it... Embrace it... It's part of your existence...

For now, the best thing you can do is to bring your awareness to your breathing...

Breathe in... Hold... And then release...

Feel the momentary relief your breathing gives... Your body needs air... And this air brings goodness inside of you... Let this positivity flow...

Breathe in... Hold... And then release...

Breathe in... Hold... And then release...

Breathe in... Hold... And then release...

Bring in more of it... Let it circulate and let it fill you... Relish the momentary relief it brings... Each breath you take diminishes the stress and the tiredness just a little bit... It makes you feel relaxed... It calms you down...

Let your heartbeat follow the rhythm of your breathing... Then try your best to slow your breathing... So that you may also slow your busy heart... Your heart needs this temporary respite as well... Give it a breather... Breathe in slowly... And do the same as you exhale... Bring in your whole self as you breathe... Be one with it... Breathe with great desire...

Breathe in... Hold... And then release...

Know that your only purpose is to be in the here and now... Acknowledge that you are tired... But bring yourself to the only place and time that matters... Be in the here and now... Achieve this with your breath... Maintain the desire and intentionality with each inhalation and exhalation...

Breathe in... Hold... And then release...

Now try to picture out your whole body... Try to conjure a mental image of your whole being... See in your mind's eye how you look like...

Go ahead and paint that picture in your mind... How do you look? More importantly, how tired do you look?

And as you imagine yourself, try to feel the tiredness that is trying to overcome you right now... How does it feel? Try to put these feelings into words... This is how you acknowledge your tiredness... This is how you tell your fatigue and stress that you know that they exist... This is the first step in trying to ease them away from you... You have to first notice that they are there... Be aware of the exhaustion that you are feeling...

Breathe in... Hold... And then release...

Know that in the here and now you are tired... And this is perfectly acceptable... The human body has its limits... And you have reached yours... Acknowledge this... This is your reality...

Try now to feel which areas of your body are particularly tired... Trace your whole being from head to foot... Start with the soles of your feet... Feel the tiredness there... And then move your way up... Move up until you reach your head... And then feel the fatigue in each of these areas...

Breathe in... Hold... And then release...

Now start to take an inventory of these areas that are particularly tired... These are the areas that have reached their limit... You might have subjected so much stress to these areas because of all the worldly demands that you have to fulfill...

Feel proud of these body parts... These are the parts that worked so hard to keep you standing... These are the body parts that allowed you to taste success... These are the parts that enabled you to be the best that you can be... So give these parts the credit that is due them... Commend them... Worship their feats of greatness... Be proud of your fatigue... It enabled you to do great things...

And now it's time to let the tiredness pass... Your body needs to rest and recover... So it's time to relieve your body of its stress... Again, be one with your breathing... Let your breathing bring you relaxation... Let your breathing sweep the stress away...

Breathe in... Hold... And then release...

Imagine that the air surrounding you as a form of energy... This energy, once taken in by the body, offers relief... It dissolves the stress away... It disintegrates the fatigue that you feel...

Breathe in... Hold... And then release...

Bring in all the energy from your environment... And then feel them work inside of you... These energies are cleansing you... They target the stress and fatigue in your body and they start to work on them... Little by little, slowly but surely, the stress and fatigue are being broken down by the energy that you breathe... So take more of it...

Breathe in... Hold... And then release...

Breathe in... Hold... And then release...

Breathe in... Hold... And then release...

Holding your breath allows this energy to flow faster inside of you... As they flow, they blow past all the stress that is precariously hanging on to your body parts... This energy sweeps them away... This energy is collecting the stress and tiredness because it will try to bring them out of you...

Breathe in... Hold... And then release...

And as you exhale, you can feel the stress and tiredness leave your body... The stress and tiredness are being carried off by your exhalation... You can feel relief from the malaise with each breath you blow out... You actually feel better now... You are starting to feel more relaxed...

Continue with the rhythm of your breathing... Breathe slowly... Do it at a pace that is unhurried... There is no need to rush... Know that relieving your body of stress takes time... Know that the process of diminishing your fatigue is a slow and methodical endeavor...

Breathe in... Hold... And then release...

Let each breath continue to bring you the good energy from your surroundings... Hold your breath and feel the energy work inside you... Feel it wipe away the stress and fatigue you feel... And then feel the delight of stress-relief after every exhalation... Allow yourself to feel more relaxed... Let calmness overcome you now... Feel your body become unburdened... It is now unshackled from the fatigue that held it down earlier... Feel the liberation... You have freedom from stress now... Relish it... Enjoy it...

Breathe in... Hold... And then release...

Breathe in... Hold... And then release...

Breathe in... Hold... And then release...

Remember to be in the only place and time that matters... You are in the here and now... And in the here and now you are being relieved of the pressure of stress... Your body is now recovering... It is resting well... It is preparing itself to do more, to achieve more...

Continue to put your thoughts and effort in your breathing... Be one with it... Bring your whole awareness to it... Your breathing is the key to achieving stress relief...

Breathe in... Hold... And then release...

And now it's time for you to return to your day... You have greatly decreased your stress levels... You are now liberated from the fatigue that bothered you... Feel the lightness of your being... You can now go back to your day with more energy...

Try to bring life back to your muscles... Move them, slowly at first... You can change your sitting position, but continue to keep your back straight... And when you are ready, open your eyes...

DAY 29—STARING AT THE MONSTER & FACING THE ANXIETIES WITHIN: GUIDED MEDITATION TO OVERCOME ANXIETY [30 MINUTES]

Close your eyes and prepare yourself... You are going on an adventure...

Are you ready? It's fine if you're not... Take your time to prepare...

It seems that you are hesitating... Don't you want to go and have this adventure? What's the adventure about, you ask? Well, you are going on a quest to quash a monster... This monster's name is Anxiety...

Oh, so that's why you hesitate... You can feel this monster within you... Do you have this monster inside of you right now? Do you have anxieties?

Ah, so it seems you have anxieties within you... This is perfectly normal... Everyone has them... That's why you are going on an adventure... Your trepidation is perfectly understandable... After all, you don't have the slightest idea of how to deal with this monster... Is this the thing that bothers you?

If it is, then worry not... I have a gift for you... It will help you in conquering your anxieties...

Here, accept my gift... This is your weapon... It is the sword of mindfulness... It's no ordinary sword... It has a special power... The power of this sword is that it can vanquish the monster within... And in order to put power in the sword, you have to be one with your breathing... Listen and follow what I say... Listen well...

Breathe in... Hold... And then release...

Do you see your sword glowing? That's because you powered it with your breath... Awareness of your breathing brings you in the here and now... The here and now is the only place and time that matters... Your weapon is at its most efficient if you bring yourself to the here and now... Let's continue to power up your sword...

Breathe in... Hold... And then release...

Breathe in... Hold... And then release...

Breathe in... Hold... And then release...

Have you noticed anything else happening to you? Do you feel more relaxed now? Try and take notice of the sensations trying to course through your body... You can actually feel your whole body getting lighter... The tension and tightness of your muscles have disappeared... This is the effect of being one with your breath... And this relaxation that you are feeling now is your armor... It is another one of my gifts to you... This armor of relaxation will protect you from the monster you will be facing off with...

Bring more power to your weapon and to your armor... Incorporate your whole desire to your breath... Concentrate and give it life... Your awareness on your breath matters... Be deliberate... Be intentional...

Breathe so that you can obtain great power... Breathe so that you can be in the here and now... This is what you will be needing as you face off with the monster...

Breathe in... Hold... And then release...

Breathe in... Hold... And then release...

Breathe in... Hold... And then release...

It is time to set foot on our journey... It's time to embark on our adventure... Get ready to meet the monster... And then do your best to vanquish it...

A little bit further and you shall reach your destination... You can now see the outline of the monster... You can see anxiety... You can see your anxieties... You didn't have to travel far and wide to find your anxieties... It's because your anxieties just reside within you...

Slowly approach the beast... Announce your arrival... Tell the beast what you intend to do with it... Tell the monster that you will vanquish it... You will make it submit... You will defeat it...

Don't be intimidated by it... It may shout and roar... It may gesture violently at you... But trust me when I tell you that it cannot hurt you... It cannot hurt you if you will not allow it to... Your anxieties need your permission and consent... If you don't give it, then it cannot do anything to you... It cannot harm you...

But you are starting to feel fear... You are fearing the unknown... You are starting to get scared of what is to come... You are thinking up adverse scenarios in your mind... This is what this monster does to you... It makes you overthink... It makes you overanalyze... It loves to bring you to a place and time that has yet to be... It likes to strip you of your confidence as it offers you glimpses of an uncertain future...

Don't allow your anxieties to do this to you... Again, it needs your consent... Banish the thought away from your mind...

Be in the here and now... Remember your weapon and your armor... Use them...

Breathe in... Hold... And then release...

Breathe in... Hold... And then release...

Breathe in... Hold... And then release...

Slay those thoughts of uncertainty... Slay those thoughts of a frightful future... They have yet to happen... They do not matter...

Breathe in... Hold... And then release...

You thrust a swift blow to the monster in front of you... It shouts in pain... It retreats... It is down, but not out... And now it starts to retaliate...

Now you are starting to feel dread again... But this time it's a different feeling that this monster is trying to throw at you... This time, the monster is making you feel regret... Regret of the past... This is your past where mistakes were made... And now you are starting to feel guilt... You look to the past with shame and embarrassment... If only you could undo things... If only you could have set things right back then...

You start to feel the heaviness of the past... This weight is pulling you down... You feel the gravity of your body being doubled... You can hardly stand... You want to fall down... You want to give in to the monster...

But do not give in... Do not give consent to it... You do not need to feel this way... Do not allow it to let you feel these emotions...

The past is done... You can no longer do anything about the past... Probably the only thing you can do is to accept them... Accept the hurt and the pain... Accept the sorrow that it brings... Accept the regret and the guilt... You cannot go back to the past and undo the hurt and the pain... But you can do something about it in the here and now...

And this is where you stand... You are in the here and now... And right here, right now, you are facing the monster... You are facing your anxieties... And you have your weapon to vanquish it... Fight the monster...

You lift your sword with both your hands, not giving in to the power of your anxieties... You raise your sword and point it at the monster... And the monster now knows that it is powerless... You have managed to overcome its tricks... You successfully brushed away the thoughts of uncertainty... You have successfully moved on from the pain of the past... Now let the blade of mindfulness pierce through the monster... It's time to crush anxiety...

Breathe in... Hold... And then release...

And down goes anxiety with one swift blow... It lies on the ground, clutching the wound that your mindfulness sword delivered... It is holding on for dear life...

You look at the eyes of the monster and you see something very familiar... The eyes you are gazing at are the same eyes as the ones on your face... They are your eyes too... You and your anxiety share the same eyes... You look at both the future and past the same... This is the truth about your anxieties... And this truth is what will liberate you... For if you share the same eyes with this monster, you can have control over what it sees...

Control... That is what you need... And know that you have it... If you do not give consent, if you do not give control to your anxieties, then it can never harm you... And you have the power to vanquish it... You just have to tap this power that is already within you...

You look at the creature that you defeated... It is no longer the scary creature that once intimidated you... In its vanquished state, you can see it for what it really is... You can see that it is surmountable... It's just a challenge you need to go through...

Just realize that all it takes for you to defeat your anxieties is the weapon of mindfulness... It's just a matter of being in the here and now... Right here, right now, your past ceases to matter... They are all but done with... Right here, right now, the future has yet to come... They also do not matter... What matters is that you exist in the present... And you have all the means to take control of your life... This is what you just did... And this is what you shall continue to do...

Breathe in... Hold... And then release...

Breathe in... Hold... And then release...

Breathe in... Hold... And then release...

Celebrate your victory... Marvel at the fact that you were able to strike down the monster that was within you... Be proud that you were able to stare through the eyes of the monster... Doing so meant that you were brave enough to do it...

Breathe in... Hold... And then release...

Continue to remain in the here and now... Continue to bring awareness to your breathing...

You are victorious... This means that the adventure is over... Congratulations on your victory... You may now return, if you wish... You shall return after the count of three...

Three...

Two...

One...

DAY 30—GUIDED SLEEP MEDITATION: OFF TO LA-LA LAND... [40 MINUTES]

Welcome to the last exercise in this book. It has been quite a ride. And to give your experience a delightful close, your last exercise will deliver you in a very restive state. This exercise will guide you so that you can be off to a place of deep slumber. Prepare yourself and in a few moments, you should be off dreaming...

Prepare your bedroom like the previous sleep exercise. Make sure that noise and other obtrusive sounds are at the minimum. Also, look into the temperature of the room—not too cold and not too hot. And then turn off the lights. Or you may just turn them down. Dim lights will also suffice for this exercise.

Lie down on your bed and get inside the covers. Attain a very comfortable position and get ready for a good night's rest. But take note that this is not just any other night of sleep. Tonight, you will be whisked away off to a far-away place.... This place is where magic exists and your fantasies become reality... You will be journeying the dream world...

Start by removing any distractions away from you... Try to eliminate thoughts that are currently haunting your mind... These things are not needed where you're going... You can perhaps remove distractions better by getting in touch with your breathing... Be mindful of your breathing... Follow its rhythm... And try to bring desire with each breath you take...

Breathe in... Hold... And then release...

Breathe in... Hold... And then release...

Breathe in... Hold... And then release...

Feel relaxation start to invade your body... Allow this relaxation to make your body feel very light... As if it's floating on air... And in fact, you are now floating... You are flying off to the sky... You are riding a cloud... It is soft and warm and fluffy... And this cloud whisks you away from your bedroom... And now you can find yourself flying off into the darkness of the night sky... You can see your house below you... A little bit higher the cloud goes and you can now see the whole town...

Let the cloud take you to a magical place... Let the cloud bring you to the world of the dreaming... Just lie down and relax... There is no need to worry... The cloud will keep you safe... It will never let you fall... You feel safe riding your cloud...

Breathe in... Hold... And then release...

And now the cloud you are riding transforms itself into a white steed... You are now riding such a majestic animal as it gallops its way to the clouds... And it slowly stops to where a rainbow is perched... Your white horse stops to let you appreciate the colors of the rainbow...

You can see the warm reds and oranges... These colors bring energy inside of you... And then you can see the calming yellows and greens... These colors bring a certain peace into your being... And of course, you can see the cool violets and blues... They give you a sense of security... The sight of these colors brings you great joy... You marvel at them and you take them all in... You try to let the rainbow penetrate your soul... It boosts your spirit...

Breathe in... Hold... And then release...

Breathe in... Hold... And then release...

Breathe in... Hold... And then release...

Your steed is slowly approaching a castle... The gates of the castle open and your white horse safely lands... You dismount your steed and slowly make your way inside... And then you realize that the castle is yours... You are the monarch that rules over this kingdom that you find yourself in... You are the ruler of your dream world...

You go inside the castle and sit on your throne... And there's a show before you... You can see in front of you all the happy memories you had... It is played before you like a movie... And this gives you great delight... You are enjoying the memories that are played out before you... All this as you sit on your throne... You start to reminisce... You start to feel a sense of longing...

You get up from your throne and start to wander off from your castle... You make your way to the inner recesses of your castle... And soon you find yourself in the treasure room... This is the room where your greatest treasure is kept... You open the treasure chest and you gaze at the treasure... This is your treasure... This is what you hold dear the most... It is there in front of you... It is safely hidden in the treasure room of your castle...

Go ahead and look at it... What does it look like? See the silhouette of your treasure... And also see all the contours, the lines, the curves, the swirls... See everything about it... What do you see? What is this treasure that you keep inside a secure treasure chest? This is something that is most important to you... And it is only you who can see it... It is only you who can appreciate its greatest value...

Breathe in... Hold... And then release...

Breathe in... Hold... And then release...

Breathe in... Hold... And then release...

It's time to close the treasure chest... You need to go out of your castle... You are yearning for an adventure... So go out and venture the far places... These are places contained in your dreaming world waiting to be discovered... And you actually have the opportunity to go to these magnificent places...

Take your white steed with you... Ride the majestic beast and feel it bring you swiftly to your destination... It takes you to a wonderful place... It is full of magical creatures... Take a few moments to take everything in... Try to see this place... Try to observe the fine details... Try to see with your mind's eye all the magnificent creatures that are present...

Gathered with you are a few people... You look around and see familiar faces... The faces you see are those of people who are close to you... These are the people that are dear to you... These are the people you care about and love...

They have gathered to let you know that they want to go with you on your journey... These people who are dear to you also yearn for the same kind of adventure that now fills your heart... And you are glad to hear this from them...

And so you and your party start preparing... You have determined that there is much more of the dreaming world to explore... You want to experience and witness the magic and splendor of the place... You and your group are heading off to la-la land...

Your adventure has started... You have instructed your group to get going... You are filled with excitement... There's a certain rush that starts to fill you... This is the joy you are getting as you dream... This is what the dreaming world gives you... Enjoy the moment... You can look forward to the great adventure that is up ahead... And you have the people that you love and care about going with you...

Your heart is filled with great contentment... You feel warm inside... You find yourself in a place that is safe... You find yourself in a place that fulfills each of your fantasies... This is the dreaming world that you find yourself in...

Feel free to continue your exploration of the dreaming world... Go ahead and take that adventure... Try to experience what the dreaming world has to offer you... Know that you own this place... Know that you are safe and secure in your own dreaming world...

And now you can start to allow the relaxation of sleep to bring you farther into the dreaming world... You are feeling so still... You are feeling so calm... You have totally let go of the waking world... In fact, nothing from the waking world exists where you are right now... Know that you are in a magical place full of wonder and excitement... And this place is yours for the taking... So go ahead and explore some more... This is your dreaming world...

You are starting to feel more and more relaxed... Everything is becoming feathery light... The waking world has finally released you from its clutches... It can no longer hold you down... You are free to be wherever you wish to be... You are free to roam and explore your dreaming world...

Breathe in... Hold... And then release...

Breathe in... Hold... And then release...

Breathe in... Hold... And then release...

Everything is quiet... everything is still... All you can hear is your heartbeat... And the faint sound of your breathing... Everything starts to fade... It starts to fade to black... Until all you see is nothing... Embrace the nothingness... Let it bring you peace...

Sleep... Sleep well... Sweet dreams... See you in the dreaming world...

www.ingramcontent.com/pod-product-compliance
Lightning Source LLC
Chambersburg PA
CBHW070101120526
44589CB00033B/1243